THE SECRET LIFE OF
JAMIE B

Ceri Worman

ORCHARD BOOKS

Contents

CHAPTER 1

Bad Publicity

Yo, what's happenin'? It's *me* – Rapstar *J.B.*!
I used to run by the name of Jamie *B.* but
now that is his-tor-*y*. I'm changing my *name*,
aiming for *fame*. Keep it simple, keep it
real – Rapstar J.B.'s the new *deal*! And I'm
cookin' up a raps to riches plan.

Yeah, I'll be fighting off the females when
my latest album goes platinum. Not to mention
the celebrity parties, the massive mansion and
the stretch limo. It's tough at the top!

So there'll be no more school and no more
boring, small town Grimly, UK for me…

*Rapstar J.B. gets ready for his latest gig,
broadcast live and happenin' from the
Hollywood Bowl to the rest of the world.*

*His dressing-room door has SUPERSTAR printed
on it in big, diamond-studded letters. But Rapstar*

J.B. hasn't let fame go to his head. After all, he is only wearing five solid gold chains round his neck and two big gold rings...per finger (...and thumb).

J.B. checks himself out in the brightly lit dressing-room mirror. His tight, white, sleeveless T-shirt shows off his sculpted six-pack. He raises one supercool eyebrow: 'Looking good, dude, looking good.'

Suddenly there's a loud banging on the door. 'Final call for Mr Rapstar J.B.!'

In two minutes the eyes of the world will be upon him. Already the fans are calling his name...

'Jamie, Jamie, get a move on! You've had all summer to sort yourself out for school and you're *still* late! Hurry up!'

Suddenly there's a banging on the bathroom door which nearly makes me swallow my toothbrush. It's Big Mo, of course; she's my minder/maid/personal assistant... Sometimes I think she forgets who's boss – the way she goes on you'd think *she* was in charge.

Back in my room it's good news: at least Big Mo's laid out my clothes for today. The bad news is, I can see a brand new school shirt, still creased from the packet. The *badder* news is that even rapstars need an education!

I put the shirt on but the collar is too big and the sleeves dangle down past my fingertips. I look like I've shrunk in the wash. Huh, you just can't get the staff these days.

Now for the school trousers and the dreaded school tie. As I knot it round my neck I can feel it strangling my originality. That's takin' liberties, man! Rappers don't wear neckties! I demand to see my lawyer.

Downstairs, Big Mo starts fussing round me like a frenzied fan.

'There now, don't you look lovely? So smart and grown-up. But you're not too old to kiss your mum goodbye now, are you?'

I lean forward and plant an air kiss at the side of each ear. It's good practice for celebrity parties.

'You know, you'll always be my little boy no matter how old you are,' she says tearfully, reaching out for a hug.

'Er, later!' I call, escaping out the front door. If she's like this when I go to school for the day, how's she going to be when I leave the country for a six-month world tour?

Just round the corner it's time for a change of image. Out of my school bag comes my hoodie, shades and beanie hat. Into the bag goes the belt I unwind from my school trousers. Now they're hanging loose and low like true baggy rapstar pants. Well, almost. Finally I clamp on my headphones – the batteries are flat but they make my ice-cool rapper image complete.

After walking into the fifth lamppost I decide to pocket the dark glasses – perhaps they're a touch shady for a cloudy morning. I'm nearly at the school gates anyway and already, hordes of excited fans are gathering inside the yard. Girls are the worst.

'*AAAAAAAAAhhhhhh!*' they scream, hugging and kissing as if they haven't seen each other for six years instead of six weeks. No doubt they'll be even more hysterical when they see *me*, Rapstar *J.B.*, so I hang back a bit.

Then I notice someone else hovering outside the school gates, too.

Rappers are sharp and this girl catches my eye for two reasons – she's a real hip-hop honey *and* she's not even in uniform, just jeans and a top. Another rebel, like me.

I head over her way. 'Yo, whassup, girl. How's it hangin'?'

'Excuse me?' The girl stares at me blankly. She's probably blown away by my rap-chat.

'The name's J.B.,' I say, 'and you are...?'

'Ah, I am sorry. I must present myself, yes? My name is Maria Ximena Valentina Constantina Diaz Rodriguez De La Silva.'

'Hmmm, you're not from round here, are you, Maria?' Rappers are *quick* and *slick*, they don't miss a *trick*.

She smiles. 'I am on student exchange, it is my first day at Grimly High.'

'No worries, girl. Welcome to my world! Stick with *me*, Rapstar *J.B.*, I'll show you *around*, what's goin' *down*. If you wanna be *cool in school*—'

Just then the bell rings and she moves

towards the gates.

'Hey, wait up!' I call after her but, as I turn, my feet catch in my ultra-baggy trousers. I stumble forward and my headphones fall off my head and somehow tangle around my knees.

Next thing I know I'm slumped on the floor like a drunk at a party and Maria's laughing louder than a polyphonic ring tone.

Then everyone in the playground turns round and joins in.

OK, so I know that rapstars always make a dramatic entrance, but this is *not* what I had in mind.

And who said there's no such thing as bad publicity?

CHAPTER 2
New Kid on the Block

'Welcome back, everyone. I hope you had a good break and are ready for work.'

Groans all round but Miss Johnson, our class tutor, just smiles brightly.

'Exciting news to start the year – we have a new girl in our class! She is visiting as part of the Worldwide Student Exchange Scheme.'

Miss Johnson's smile gets even brighter.

'Maria is from a small country in South America,' she continues. 'This gives you all a chance to practise the Spanish you learned last year—'

Everyone's talking at once now:

'What Spanish we learned last year?'

'If we're nice to her we might get to go to South America on a school trip!'

Suddenly Maria is standing in the doorway and someone wolf-whistles. She looks terrified as she scans the sea of strange faces, but then she catches my eye and she actually...giggles. Huh, the girl's got no respect! Why'd she have to end up in my class?

'OK everyone, I'd like someone to be Maria's buddy for the day and show her to her lessons—'

'Me, Miss!'

'I'll show 'er round.'

There's no way I want to be with Maria. She's already destroyed my public image. I look down and pretend to read, but my stomach is sinking faster than a Christmas hit in the January charts.

'James Bradshaw.'

I knew it.

'Or should I say, "B., Jamie B. the Superspy?"'* She steers Maria towards me saying, 'This young man was on the front page of the local newspaper this summer, for helping to keep law and order on our streets! He's the perfect choice to show you around. Sit next to him – I'm sure you'll be in safe hands.'

*Footnote: To find out more about Jamie B. the Superspy, read the first adventure in the Secret Life of Jamie B.

The whole class whistles and claps but, for once, I don't want to take a curtain call. Why is it that, with Maria around, my fans lose total respect? I don't look at her when she sits down. Sometimes even rapstars want their privacy.

'Now, Saima and Ben, please give out the year planners while I write the timetable on the board. Then you can all copy it down *carefully* and *quietly*. I don't want to hear any talking.'

Five minutes later, everyone's *carefully* scribbling away and *quietly* whispering about what they did in the holidays. I still haven't looked at Maria, but suddenly she grips my arm and hisses, 'What did the teacher mean – *Superspy*?'

'Oh, nothing, just some trouble in the 'hood, but I sorted it,' I mumble. 'That's history now, anyway. I've had a career change since then.'

'But what happened? I must know, it's very important—'

'Too much noise, class!' Miss Johnson suddenly shouts.

Everyone shuts up and I carry on practising my autograph. I can't decide on J.B. or Jay Bee...

'Yes, early rap lyrics signed by Rapstar J.B. himself, ladies and gentlemen. This is what Snootly's Auction House proudly presents for auction tonight as Lot Number One. Now, if you will permit me, I will read out a few lines from this creative genius.'

The auctioneer puts on some discreet, half-moon spectacles, and fixes his bow-tie. Then, in a cut-glass English accent, he starts to read.

'A-hem... Yo,
Every day we hesitate / half past eight / at the school gate
Not to mention the detention you get for being late
They clone us in school uniform / classes dull a chloroform
But listen-up it's not for long
Yeah, listen-up it's not for long
'Cos me and my rap song / are gonna shake up a storm!'

*

Loud cheers rip through the dark-suited, furs-and-pearls audience. The auctioneer wipes his forehead with a large handkerchief and bows modestly.

'Thank you, ladies and gentleman and may I say, big-up the Snootly's Massive! Now, who will start us in the bidding? Do I hear twenty thousand...?'

The air is filled with a forest of hands.

'Everyone has their hand up to show they've finished, except you, Jamie! It's almost the end of the lesson, so I hope you *have* copied the timetable down?'

'Word perfect, Miss,' I say, slamming my planner shut before it can be used in evidence against me.

Miss Johnson smiles briefly. 'Well done. Now you can show Maria to your next class...'

Right on cue, the bell rings and everyone heads for the door. 'Come on, Maria,' I say as she packs her stuff away. 'Just follow me.'

Out in the corridor I try to look as if I know where I'm going.

'We have English now, in room B17,' Maria tells me, as we struggle against the crowd outside.

'I know that,' I say irritably, wondering why everyone is surging towards us. Perhaps they're autograph hunting *again*.

Maria grabs my arm, and turns me around. She's got the grip of a well-trained bouncer and she's not letting me go. I think she likes me!

Her dark brown eyes look deep into mine and then she speaks, 'Jamie, room B17 – it is *this* way.'

CHAPTER 3

Lost for Words

'You're tuned into Goss TV for the latest chat. And tonight we're outside the new and exclusive Hip-Hoppodrome Club. It's the opening night and all the biggest and baddest celebs are here.'

(The camera zooms in on a s-t-r-e-t-c-h limo as it parks up next to the red carpet.)

'Wow, that's the longest limo eva! And out steps Rapstar J.B. – who else? – with his latest hip-hop honey...'

(Close-up on Rapstar J.B. and Maria X as they walk up the red carpet, waving to the screaming fans.)

'My, but don't they look a lovely couple! And here comes the club owner, Mr Goldchain, to greet *them – it's such an honour for him to have Rapstar J.B. here tonight!'*

(The cameras start flashing as Mr Goldchain opens the club door. Then he steps forward to say a few words of welcome...)

'Stop straggling in the corridor. The lesson has started!' Mr Turner is bellowing at us from the classroom doorway.

Maria scuttles in and sits down at an empty desk, right under the teacher's nose. Typical. I usually go for the back row, but there's an empty seat next to her and she points for me to sit there. I can't help it – I just have this effect on girls.

When I do park my booty next to hers, she whispers urgently, 'It is important we speak in private. We will talk later, yes? I want to ask—'

'OK everyone, no talking, stop chattering, BE QUIET!' Mr Turner begins – he never uses one word or phrase where three will do.

'That's better. Now I want you to make up a poem, a verse, an ode about where you live.'

He smiles. Everyone groans. He asked us to do this last year so I guess he's still working to his old timetable, but I'm not about to tell him. Rapstars know when it's best to *lip it* or *zip it*.

I look round the class. Some people have brought their old English books and are copying last year's poem out again. I haven't got mine, but I'm buzzin' with ideas. I put my hand up.

'Can we write a rap, Mr Turner?'

'Hmm...I believe rap lyrics use the three 'r's – rhythm, rhyme and repetition? So...yes. Great. Very good. Excellent.'

Typical! Mr Turner has managed to make rap – the poetry of *da street* – sound like a worthwhile school exercise! No way...

After half an hour, and six crossed out pages of my English book, I've only come up with three lines of rap – and even two of those are repeated. Mind you, every word is so-solid gold. Even the full stops are silver.

And I'm not the only one having a hard time, either.

'Sir, I'm stuck.'

'I can't do this!'

'What good's *poetry* when you leave school?'

'Mr Turner, can we work with a friend?' someone suddenly asks.

I expect Mr Turner to say no, but he jumps at the idea. 'Wonderful...yes, collaborate, co-operate, participate! OK, class, get into groups and I want you to work with one, no – two, no – three friends.'

Of course! I get into a group with my homies, Ben, Marcus and Deepak while Maria is claimed by three girls. They all huddle and giggle and then one of them, Big-Mouth Elysha, comes over to borrow a pencil sharpener. I'm sure she's spying on us because there's a lot of whispering when she goes back to the others – and even more giggling. Big yawn – it's so *uncool* to act *da fool.*

'Right, class, it's time to hear some work in progress from your groups. Choose a spokesperson to read out your poem, perform it, make it come alive!'

Laura Pratt shoots her hand up straight away.

'Aah, Laura, thank you. Tell us the title of your group's poem.'

'Sir, can I go to the toilet, sir?'

'Hmm, original title, Laura, but—'

'Sir, it's *urgent!*'

'Well, read us your poem first, Laura. Then you can go to the toilet, the bathroom, the Ladies.'

Laura stands up, crosses her legs and reads the title aloud, '"Why We Love Grimly"...'

Right on cue, someone starts up a really noisy lawnmower just outside the classroom window, so luckily I am saved from all but the last few lines,

'...And best of all is Saturday,
when we all go out to play,
take our money down the shops
to buy some mags and lollipops.'

Laura makes a dash for the door.

'Lovely, delightful, charming, don't you agree, class?' Mr Turner says just as *someone* makes a vomiting noise.

'Bradshaw!'

'Sir, I was just clearing my throat,' I say innocently.

'Then you'll be ready to razzle, dazzle and amaze us with your rap poem, won't you?'

My homies begged me to do the rappin' of course, but now that it actually comes to the moment I don't feel right. My arms and legs are twitching like a break dancer's and the classroom seems as hot as a tropical nightclub.

Maybe I'm coming down with a fever? I stand up and loosen my tie which makes everyone cheer and makes me feel even hotter...*whassup?* I've got to do this, they're all looking my *way* – it's time for my *say*.

'Er..."Grimly Rap"...

'Yo... It ain't so hot / livin' in Grimly
It ain't so hot / livin' in Grimly
New York, London, Harlem / Is what it's not
I said it ain't so...'

Out of the corner of my eye I catch Maria yawning and my voice fades out like someone pulled the plug on a mic.

Before I can recharge, Big-Mouth Elysha suddenly lets rip, 'Sir, sir, we've got a rap, too. Can our group go next? Please, sir!'

I look up to see Mr Turner nod his head, then they all start whispering, 'Go on Maria!', 'You go, girlfriend!', 'Go! Go!'

CHAPTER 4
Rival Rapper

Maria stands up and *moves* to *da groove* as she launches into her rap.

'Yo, Mr J.B., you don't in-ter-est me
With your grisly grim stories of your town
  Grimly

'Sure, back home the best things in life are free
That's sun and fun and friends and family
And we love our cities, our towns / we love
  our country!
But we can't forget about the poverty

'So, you're crazy – *loco* – to complain, J.B.
'Cos it AIN'T so grim in your hometown,
  Grimly.'

Maria's makin' a BIG NOISE and her hair is bouncing around in corkscrew curls. When she stops all the girls go wild, cheering and clapping.

Yes, Maria's electric and I'm suffering from shock! She never told me she could *talk the talk*. She never told me she could *chat the chat*. She never told me she could *rap the rap*! And to think Rapstar J.B.'s been showing her around, tellin' her what's going down – Maria X., my new rival rapper!

Well, no more Mr Nice Guy. The Comeback Kid is in town and the battle is *on*.

Some of the boys start whispering, 'Go on, J.B.! You show 'em!' Then Mr Turner nods at me and I stand up.

There's no stopping me this time. I'm ready to rumble with Maria and her crew for disrespecting our rap. I have to make it up on the spot, freestyle, but that's no problem for a rapstar like me…

'Yo, it ain't so cool / living in Grimly
It AIN'T so cool / living in Grimly
Nuthin' to see, nuthin' to do
Only a fool / yeah, only a FOOL

Um…Sitting on a STOOL / er…mad as
    a…mule
Likes living in Grimly!'

The rap's really flowing now and the stunned silence tells me that everyone is blown away by my talent. I'm on a roll and it's time to end my killer rap with a BIG finish…

'Get that clearly, do you hear me?
One more time, check out my cool rhyme
No one likes living in Grimly
And I ain't talking dim…ly
'Cos we don't even have a GYM…ly…'

There's a bit of a pause – probably out of respect for my genius – but then Ben, Marcus and Deepak start cheering, and all the boys join in.

Then the bell goes – but is it for the end of the lesson or the end of round one? We eyeball each other across the classroom – Rapstar J.B. *v* Maria X. – rival rappers!

Mr Turner is spluttering with excitement. 'Poetry slam, class – that's what just happened –

a spontaneous poetry slam!'

He's still muttering as we crowd out of the doors, 'I must tell the Head of English – I'll put their names down for that competition she mentioned the other day...'

Out in the corridor I remember I'm supposed to be showing Maria where to go next. When I look back in the classroom she's still at her desk, copying down some notes in her school planner. Bad move – rappers don't take x-tra notes. No good for the street cred.

I linger at the door like a stalker on a stake-out. Maria must be feeling crushed after our battle of words and I even start to feel sorry for her. Besides, the next lesson is Science and she might know where it is.

At last she packs her books away and joins me in the corridor. 'We are in Lab 17 next,' she says. (Nice one.) 'We will walk together, no? I must make a deal with you.'

I'm too surprised to say anything. A deal? What is she talking about? Maybe she wants to buy my rap lyrics and cash in on my fame? No chance.

We cross the school yard, away from the

crowds. Maria continues, 'Jamie, I will propose to you an exchange.'

'Exchange?'

'Yes,' she smiles. *Hmmm*, she's even prettier when she does that. 'You do something for me and I do something for you.'

Then she grips my arm, *again*. OK, there's nothing I like more than a friendly fan but a super rapstar has to play it safe. After all, the word *fan* is short for *fanatic* and Maria does have a scary gleam in her eye. Next thing you know she'll be camping outside my house!

'Hold up, Maria...er, I don't see how you can help *me* with anything.'

'Really?' she says, looking surprised. 'Isn't it obvious I can help you with your raps? Then you can help me because I have a *big* problem. Miss Johnson said you are a superspy, no?'

'No. Don't you listen? That was just um...a holiday job. And anyway, what makes you think I need help with my raps?'

'Oh, come on, Jamie. In the English class just now, you know?'

'J.B.! The name's J.B. And what? *What* do I know?'

Maria puts her head to one side, thinking hard, 'Now what did Elysha say? Ah, *si*, your *rap* was *crap*.'

Talk about disrespect! Once again I'm lost for words. Well, not really. I've got plenty of words to describe Maria.

Unfortunately, they're all PARENTAL ADVISORY (18+) and I can't say them out loud.

CHAPTER 5

So You Think You're a Rapstar?

Maria stalks me all day after that, but I give her the silent treatment and she finally gets the message. That girl is bad news!

By the time I get home from school, later, I'm feeling a bit down – like a rapstar whose career is on the skids. Not that Maria has anything to do with it, of course. She's got a *big* problem all right – jealousy of my superior rap style. Though she wasn't that bad...for a beginner.

Big Mo serves me tea and I do the washing up. It's her job really, but she's found a legal loophole that gives her power over my money until I'm eighteen, so I don't get my weekly allowance if I refuse.

Even after all my hard work slaving over hot soap suds, homework and watching TV, I can't sleep, so I flick through a music mag just to check out the competition. Then a quiz catches my eye:

✳ So you think you're a Rapstar? ✳

Try this quiz and see if you should be RAPPING up on stage or PACKING up your ideas for a Rapstar career.

Yo! I already *know* the answer but, just to prove it, I pick up a pen and get ready for my date with fame and fortune.

1. Are you:
❏ a) Cool?
❏ b) Hot?
❏ c) Frozen?

This quiz must have seen me coming! When you're Rapstar J.B. and you're already cooler than ice then the answer is obvious.

☑ c) Frozen?

2. Are you:
- ❏ a) Fast-talking?
- ❏ b) Fast-moving?
- ❏ c) Fast and loose?

Ha! A trick question. You gotta be fast-talking *and* fast-moving to be a rapstar, so if you choose just one you lose! I am quick-talking, quick-moving *and* my clothes are *baggy wi'out bein' saggy*. Easy.

☑ c) Fast and loose?

3. Some rappers talk with an accent. Choose one:
- ❏ a) American
- ❏ b) London
- ❏ c) Other

My accent is unique, it makes me stand out from the crowd. It's Yamerican (Yorkshire-American). OK, so I live in Yorkshire but, *hey!*, I watch *The Simpsons* every day!

☑ c) Other

4. Do you wear:
❏ a) Bling?
❏ b) Bling Bling?
❏ c) Bling Bling Bling?

Yeah, this will really trip up the phoneys. Being a rapstar, I know all the rapspeak. Bling means bright things. I *always* wear a so-solid gold necklace, ring and bracelet (or at least I will, when I've saved up my allowance). That's three bright things which make me…

☑ c) Bling Bling Bling?

All 'c's – now to read the results and take my rightful place as the King of Rap. I turn to page 27.

<u>Answers:</u>
Mostly 'a's Yowser! Keep on rapping.
Mostly 'b's Respect! Keep on rhyming…you're on your way up.
Mostly 'c's Get outta here and change career!

Well, what do stupid quizzes prove anyway? A one-off like me will never fit into their stupid boxes!

By now it's nearly midnight and I'm still wide awake. I'll show those magazine editors *and* Maria. Time to get up and work on some fresh and funky rap lyrics.

I switch on my bedside light and pull out my golden notebook from the bottom of my school bag: the one with Rapstar J.B. Rap Lyrics - Listen-up to what's written up! on the front.

My mind runs free and the ideas flow. It's easy...

Rapstar J.B. is exploding with ideas. He writes on everything around him – the silk sheets on his bed, the walls of his mansion, the shells of his two pet turtles... And if he can't get his hands on anything else, he writes on his own skin!

Right now he's penning his new album and the raps are really flowing – up one arm, across his chest and down both legs.

His agent had a massive body-photocopier

custom-made for J.B. to use as a bed. He switches it on every night. Music mags have said this is X-tra X-treme but J.B. has learned from his mistakes. Some time back he went into a writing frenzy and wrote lyrics all over himself. The best rap songs eva!

He wrote day and night, non-stop, then – tired, dazed and confused – he took a long hot shower to relax...and washed those platinum lyrics right down the plughole.

Whoosshhhhhh...gurgle!

J.B. desperately inspected his whole body, hoping that at least one genius rhyme had survived. But only one WORD remained – on his ankle, where the soap had missed. This precious, original, multi-million-dollar word had two letters and an exclamation mark...

Yo!...that's it, my first word already and I'm totally buzzin'! Hang on, what's this?

Press pause.

I look down at the page just where I was about to write my first (so-solid) word, but someone has beaten me to it. I read what it says...

¡Ayuda! ¡Help me find my sister, Jamie!
Maria.

Whoa – too many exclamation marks. She's really pumping up the volume! Find her sister? What sister? Does Maria really have a problem, like she said?

But when I think back to this afternoon I get totally fired-up. This girl is some kind of psycho-stalker! She already tried to get my attention by going on about her *big* problem, and when that didn't work she obviously sneaked into my school bag and wrote graffiti in my notebook! Even then, she t the name wrong. ¡¡It's J.B.!!

I bet she's really after my dynamite raps and she's just playing me with this sistery-story. And am I going to fall for it? *No way, José*...er, I mean, *No fear, Maria*.

Now my creative flow has flown away. I give up on the writing and switch off the light. At last I fall asleep and dream of performing a 'Revenge Rap' – with rave reviews.

CHAPTER 6

Revenge Rap

SINGLES HIT LIST

Rapstar J.B.'s 'Revenge Rap'
*Star rating: * * * * * (a future classic)*

J.B. is so hot right now he has to sleep in the freezer. He's so on fire, his new rap leaves you with third-degree burns!

Revenge Rap is a mix of hip-hop/rap with a unique Yorkshire vibe from the streets of Grimly. And it's sure to be another hit for the rapstar.

Listen-up as J.B. spits words like daggers at rival rapper, Maria X. (She strikes fear into the heart of the tuffest Rapstar – 'nuff said!) Here's a sample:

I'm warning you now that my words might offend
But that's what it's like when you're driven to the end.
Of the line / now I'm fine / but I'll tell you a story
'Bout a time in my life when it wasn't all glory
When Maria said she 'beat' me in a rap slam
Well, she would say that, she's her own Number One fan!
But that girl is falser than chips with no salsa
Yeah, that girl is faker than a fake tan...

Turn it UP! You wanna hear more? Don't stress. Get it X-press. To order your copy now, pick up the phone, listen for the dial tone and press those keys, *bleep bleep...*

Bleep! Bleep! Bleep! Bleep! Bleep! Bleep!

'Jamie, your alarm clock's been going off for ages. Wake up!'

I open my eyes and *Aaaaggh!* Big Mo is looming over me like a lawsuit and she's waving a piece of paper in my face.

'Jamie, you're late and what's this?' she demands.

'M-my new m-multi m-million-dollar recording contract?' I m-mumble into the pillow.

'No. It's a note from school. How many times have I told you to give school notes straight to me – not leave them squashed at the bottom of your bag?!'

'Call my lawyers, that's invasion of privacy!'

'No it's not, it's sorting you out. So, do you want me to sign it?'

'What*ever...*' It's far too early in the morning to decide, let Big Mo take care of it – what are staff for, anyway?

Fast forward: I actually *run* to school, and risk ruining my rapstar street cred, but I still get there ten minutes after the bell has gone.

'Note, please,' says the school secretary as I walk into the building. I hand over the note that Big Mo signed.

'Now write your name here, please,' she adds, pushing a book towards me. I sigh; these autograph hunters are everywhere. Still, you can't disappoint your fans, can you?

'And hurry up with the Late Book, Jamie, someone else is waiting!'

I sign 'J.B.' with my special gold pen and set off down the corridor. Just then, someone calls out my name and I *know* it's not another adoring fan.

'Bradshaw!'

'Yo, sir?'

'You are late for assembly, Bradshaw, and stop all that yo-ho-ho-ing. You sound like a pirate.'

'Yes, Sir.' You have to feel sorry for Mr Nail – he's stuck in a time-warp from five centuries ago.

'Now hurry up, lad. It's a special assembly. Something about a poetry competition which, I believe, you've been entered for.'

A competition! What competition? But Mr Nail doesn't stop to chat – he escorts me to assembly like he's my very own personal bodyguard. Maybe I'll offer him a job; it's bound to pay better than teaching.

We get to the assembly just as Mr Turner walks on stage.

'Good morning, everyone.'

'*Good mor-ning, Mr Tur-ner.*'

'Or should I say, *bon matin, guten tag...buenos dias?* Yes, I'm using three languages this morning because we have a visitor from the Richard English Language School – none other than Mr English himself, in person, in the flesh!'

A few people clap (mainly the teachers) and then all the lights snap off and we're plunged into darkness.

A gravelly voice fills the hall: 'Yo, kids, are you ready for a fight?'

No response. This isn't turning out to be a typical school assembly *at all.*

A spotlight suddenly hits the stage and lights up a flashy white-suited figure. 'No worries,' he growls. 'I'm not talking fists, I'm talking verbals.

A poetry slam! A battle of words with the kids from my school. It's cool.'

He's trying to talk the talk like he's the King o' Bling – but he's all wrong. Everything about him is false. He's got blond-streaked hair and he's OD'd on the fake tan. I need my shades to cut out the glare from his bright orange skin and over-the-top, fake gold jewellery. He ain't *flashy* – just *trashy*.

'We get kids from all over the world coming to learn English at our school. And we want everyone to see what a fantastic job we're doing! So what better way to show off their word-power than by holding a rap contest? 'Course we're making it worth *your* while to enter by offering a prize of…'

He pauses for effect and his face shines with sweat. He stands there, popping out of his shirt like a burger from a bun as he chomps on a fat cigar. The room is hushed as everyone strains to hear the magic words.

'…five hundred *pesos*!'

Suddenly we're all talking at once, like reporters at a press conference.

'Does he mean money?'

'How much is that worth, then?'

'That's not what they use in Monopoly, is it?'

'Be quiet, No Talking, SILENCE!' I'll say this for Mr Turner, he does try – but everyone's too excited to shut up. Finally he gives in: 'Right, well, that's the end of the assembly, then. And a big thank you to Mr English. *Merci, danke...gracias.*'

Mr Bling smiles a whiter-than-white smile (false smile, bleached teeth) and he doesn't stop until there's a camera flash! Then he grabs the mic and his voice booms out over the hall: 'Don't forget, kids. This is a chance to show off your talents and see if you can beat my students. It's an offer you can't refuse.' He's got the sort of voice you wouldn't want to meet in a dark alley.

Suddenly there's this fluttering, flickering sound and hundreds of leaflets come flying down from the roof. I've got to admit it, the man's a publicity genius. I wonder if he'll agree to be my agent?

Then I scrape a leaflet off my nose and read...

The Richard English Language School
presents its first ever

POETRY SLAM!

A battle of wits where no one gets hurt!
Performance poetry – rap, hip-hop
and spoken word.

All contestants must use the theme of
FREEDOM – because learning a language
breaks down barriers and sets you free!

To take place at the new Richard English
Language School, Sheffield.
Friday 15th September 6.30 pm

Open to anyone aged 9-15

❋WARNING❋
No insults
No bad language

I can't believe my eyes. NO insults? NO bad language? What kind of battle is that? They're the main ingredients for my 'Revenge Rap' (subtitle: 'Set J.B. free/get Maria outta here!'). I have to get out of this contest now or my rapstar rep will be yesterday's news.

But before I can take action Miss Johnson appears in front of me with Maria at her side. They're both smiling at me like a pair of magazine cover girls.

'Jamie, this has all worked out so well!' Miss J. says happily. 'Please thank your mother for giving Maria a place to stay while she's in England.'

A place to stay? I look at her blankly and she waves a familiar piece of paper in front of me.

'Your mother signed a note which you handed in to the secretary this morning, remember? We had a number of offers but Maria chose yours, so I'll bring her round this evening.'

Whoa! What is it with Maria? She just won't get off my *case* – checking into my *space* – moving into my *place* – I can't stand her *pace*!

Next time Big Mo signs a contract for me, I'll *definitely* check the small print myself.

CHAPTER 7
Taking Over Da House

'It's a lovely day, rise and shine!' Big Mo tugs at the curtains and the sun strikes me like a spotlight.

'*Mmphhh* it's Saturday morning. I don't *do* Saturday mornings!' I hide under the covers like a publicity-shy superstar.

'Jamie, get up and greet your guest or no pocket money for the rest of your life!'

'J.B., the name's J.B.! And that's *blackmail*!'

'Well, it's either that or The Wet Flannel – your choice.'

What's goin' down? Is Big Mo really threatening me? I could fire her for that... On the other hand, she has been with me for years. Perhaps I'll humour her, just this once. 'OK, OK, give me two minutes.'

When I get downstairs the table is set and Big Mo is cookin' up bacon and eggs. That's more like it: at least I get the rapstar treatment in the kitchen department.

But as soon as I slump at the table, Big Mo and Maria gang up on me.

'So, you're taking Maria to the shopping mall,' Big Mo starts.

I nearly choke on a piece of toast. What has Maria been saying? Spend my Saturday in a shopping mall? I'd rather head-bang to heavy metal on a brick wall.

'I wish I could come too, but Saturday's the busiest day at the salon,' she continues.

'Yeah, I wish I could come with you, Maria, but Saturday's the busiest day on TV,' I say sadly.

'Jamie!' Big Mo bangs a plate down on the table and starts talking in italics. '*Of course* you'll take *Maria* out. She wants to meet up with her *sister*. You know; the one who works in a shop in *Sheffield*.'

'What sister? What shop?' This is making as much sense as the small print on a record contract.

'Oh, Jamie. You never listen, do you? Maria's sister is on an Earn as You Learn study trip.

She's based at the Richard English Language School. Apparently you've both been entered into a poetry contest there?'

'Rap,' I say. 'Not poetry, it's rap. A rap *slam!*'

'I think he is having *una broma* – a joke, Señora Bradshaw,' Maria interrupts sweetly. 'Jamie said we will take the bus to Sheffield. There I will see my sister in the mall and buy presents for my family. And he wants to buy you a present that is very special for letting me stay.'

'*Really?* Well, that *is* a surprise.' Big Mo softens. 'You know, Maria, I think you're having a good influence on Jamie already!'

Huh, I'm outnumbered by an all-girl crew in my own home.

As soon as Big Mo's back is turned Maria whispers to me, '*Gracias*, I knew you would help me and my sister! That is why you wanted me to stay, no?'

And before I can think of a comeback she's clicked on the TV…

'Yo! This is da Massive Chart Show, bringing you the nation's favourite hits on RapTV. Check it out!

'And it looks like we got a new entry in the charts, but will it knock Rapstar J.B. off his ten-week, Number One spot? Well, here he is in the studio, so let's find out what he thinks!'

(The presenter passes the mic to a cool-looking J.B.)

'Yo, I ain't gonna be beat by no feisty female crew! J. B.'s Number One and they'll be Number Two!'

(He hands the mic back to the presenter who yells into it...)

'All-right, let's see what the public says. And at Number Two we have...listen up...'Revenge Rap' by Rapstar J.B.! You're going down, J.B.!'

(A trap door opens on the stage and the rapstar disappears into the darkness below.)

'Noooooooooo!'
  'And the new Number One top-selling hit across the nation is..."We're Taking Over Da House!" by

Da Sinista Sistas. Give it up, 'cos here they are now!'

(Waaaaah! Big Mo and Maria X. come screaming onto the stage ready to perform, hugging and kissing each other in excitement at the news...)

Kiss! 'Goodbye, Mrs Bradshaw.' *Kiss! Kiss!* 'I am so happy we go to Sheffield. See you later.' Maria is standing on the doorstep and kissing Big Mo goodbye on the cheek *three* times.

'Yeah, later!' I say, giving Big Mo a casual wave. After all, we are practically out on the street in full view of the fans.

'Do you always do that,' I ask as we head for the bus stop, 'even when you'll see someone again in a few hours?'

'Oh yes, in my country we kiss friends, family, even teachers, every time when we meet or say goodbye. You don't do that here?'

I shake my head.

'Ah *si*, I forget. You Eenglish are so cold,' she says, half-smiling.

'I think you'll find the word is cool,' I say. 'Or, in my case, supercool.'

Then I clamp on my headphones. End of conversation.

CHAPTER 8

Who's That Girl?

Two hours later and Rapstar J.B. can be found trailing after a Spanish shopaholic in a Sheffield shopping mall. This is all wrong! I should be in a recording studio right now, laying down a track for my new album. Instead I feel like just laying down.

'Wait up, Maria. Look, we've bought our presents, it's time for a rest,' I start to cough weakly.

'But, my sister, there are more shops here to visit—'

'Food…drink…can't go on…' I croak, collapsing onto a convenient café stool.

'OK, you sit down, Jamie. I will go all alone. I will find my sister and you can eat your…your Eenglish cream tea.'

Huh, she thinks she can savage me with sarcasm. No chance. I stay ice-cube cool. 'So you don't know *exactly* which shop your sister works in, Maria?'

'No…she—'

'*Whoa*, hold it right there. If we're gonna case every shop in the mall then I definitely need some body fuel first.'

Maria looks angry. 'No, you don't understand, she—'

'Talk to the hand…' I say, holding it in front of my face, and I swear she stamps her foot in anger. A definite diva!

'*Bueno.* I will look in those shops over there. In ten minutes I come back.' Then she puts her bag on a chair next to mine saying, 'You will take care of this, no?'

'No…I mean, yes. It'll be safe with me. Rappers don't miss nuthin', girl. Catch ya later.'

Why all this drama about meeting up with her sister?, I think, as I grab a drink and chill out in a comfy chair. It's very warm in the shopping centre and the mall chill-out muzak is so blaah and boring that I can feel my eyelids closing just for a…*zzzzzzzz*

*

Rap Star J.B. is dozing backstage after another crowd-pleasing concert.

His minder nudges him awake and holds an ice-cold can of Coke up to J.B.'s lips. His bling-team rush forward to polish up his gold. J.B.'s make-up artist doesn't have much to do (how can you improve on perfection?) but keeps busy by patting his face with a warm fluffy towel, while his personal stylist files his nails.

The rapstar sighs and clears his throat. Everyone stops what they are doing. They wait, in awe, for words that are sure to be deep and from the street...

'It takes stress to express and I ain't messin'...'
Everyone nods respectfully. 'Uh, huh.'

Rapstar J.B. continues: 'Yeah, rappin' is hard work, man, you get my message? But I don't need no chill-pill, just my neck massage.'

He clicks his fingers and a beautiful babe steps forward. She puts her hands on his shoulders and murmurs...

'Jamie, wake up! *Dónde está?* Where is it?'

Someone is shaking me, hard, and I'd know

that stranglehold grip anywhere. '*W-Whassup? Whaassappening?* I yell, coming round from my shopping-mall coma to see Maria's face in 3D close-up.

'My bag. You are playing the hide and seek?'

'No, honest, it was here. I never took my eyes off it! Well...er, maybe for a second...'

Maria's voice is suddenly stereophonic. 'My money, my photos, my *pasaporte!*'

'Your pass-a-port? I mean, your passport? Why did you have that in your bag?'

Her eyes flash in annoyance. 'It is the ID. For sure you must have ID! In my country you can be arrested without ID.'

Press pause: If Maria has lost her passport she can't leave the country. We'll have to adopt her and I'll be outnumbered by females for ever!

Press play: 'Your bag – we must find it!' I say urgently.

Instinctively I reach for my headphones. The batteries are still flat but I need some quiet to think. If only Big Mo was here – no one would dare to take on Rapstar *J.B.,* with his very own personal se-cur-it-*y*.

Yo! That's it! A big place like this must have security guards. I grab the mall-map off Maria and scan the page.

'Come on, *Maria*, I've got an *idea*!' (Ha! I'm a poet and don't I know it.)

The security guard's office is buzzin'. There are banks of CCTV screens everywhere, zooming in and out, like it's a TV recording studio. I am *so* at home here! We tell the guard what happened and he takes pity on Maria and makes her a hot, sweet cup of tea.

'There you are, luv. Nowt like a cuppa to cheer you uppa.'

Huh, everyone's a rapper these days.

'Now then, we've 'ad a lot of petty crime in the mall these last few months. Bag snatchers, pickpockets and suchlike. Let's play the video tape back and see if we can find out what happened to your bag.'

He presses a few buttons, then a face that I know and love appears on the screens – it's me!

So there I am, looking cool in my baggy jeans and hoodie, and there's Maria, mall-map in hand, marching off. OK, so the film's in cheapo black-and-white but it has a certain gritty, urban style. I'll bear that in mind for my next music video.

Wait a minute – what's this? A boy and a girl giving out business cards in the mall. Now they're sitting down at the table next to mine. She's quite fit, why didn't I notice *her*? Oh, yeah, I can see why – my eyes are closed.

Now she's taking off her jacket and putting it over the stool with Maria's bag on it. She's looking all around. She's standing up again and picking up her coat...along with Maria's bag. All in one clean sweep! Seriously shady! Then the girl and boy are walking away and off camera.

'Nice work, that,' the security guard nods. Then he sees Maria's stricken face. 'Oops, sorry, luv. Let's just print that out for you.' And with a flick of a switch, there's a grainy black-and-white print of the girl, the boy and a dozing J.B. – my first poster!

The guard hands it to Maria, who is still wide-eyed. She stares at it and a name escapes from her lips like a sigh, 'Sofia!'

'You what, luv?'

Maria looks dazed. 'How could she do that? Impossible!'

He shakes his head. 'Aye it's unbelievable, isn't it? No shame, thieves like them.' Then he gets out a pen and a piece of paper. 'Now then, if you'll just make a statement, I'll phone the police.'

Maria jumps up as if she's just had an electric shock.

'Police? No. Never. I... Thank you *señor*, but this is only a storm in a cup of tea. I must go now, I have to...'

And she's off.

I look at the security guard and shrug my shoulders. 'Er...she's from South America,' I say, before setting off after Maria.

I finally catch sight of her heading into the underground car park.

'Hey, Maria, what's going down?' I yell.

At first I think she's not going to stop but she finally slows and turns to face me. She looks frightened and her voice is a whisper. 'Please, you must tell no one. That girl. That...thief. She is my sister. Sofia!'

CHAPTER 9
Urban Trash

'Is that the big problem – your sister's a bag snatcher? Is that what you meant when you said she worked here…?'

'No!' The word echoes round the car-park like a shot. 'Something is wrong. She came here to study. Sofia is not a thief. I don't understand!'

'*You* don't understand? Ha! Welcome to *da club*, Maria!'

Her eyes widen and her shoulders start shaking. Just for a moment, I think she's laughing and then I realise she's not. She's crying.

'What is happening?' she mumbles, turning her face away from me. 'It was our dream to come here…'

And now she's crying even harder, so with rapstar cool, I reach forward to comfort her. But at the same time she turns around and somehow

I end up with my finger in her eye. *Whoa!* Where's the rewind button when you need it?

I wait for her to calm down a bit and risk patting her hand (not sure if that's in *Da Rapstar Book of Moves* but at least it's safe). Then I try asking a question, to distract her from the pain.

'So, er...you wanna tell me the whole story?'

She dabs her eyes with a tissue and suddenly the words are tumbling out.

'We are so happy, Jamie. First, I win top prize at my school – to come on the exchange to England. My family can never afford this themselves, you know? And it's important to learn English really well to get a good job in our country.

Sofia wants to come with me, but she is working to save up for university, so it is impossible. Then she finds out about a very cheap study trip to Sheffield with the Richard English School. It's perfect!'

She blows her nose and I'm thinking that *perfect* is not the word I'd choose to describe Richard English (aka Mr Bling).

She carries on: 'My sister signs up for Earn as

You Learn so she can come to England for six months. You can then study English and they find for you a place to live and a proper job to pay for the course too. She came last month. And I chose to come to Grimly High on my exchange to be near Sofia, so we can meet.'

'So why didn't you just visit her at the Richard English School?'

'*This* is my problem. It is so strange. Every time I phone, from my country and here in England, they say Sofia is out working and call back later. She is never at school and she never calls me – and I do not know where she is staying. But then she sends me a postcard with a photo of this mall on it. She only signs her name – nothing more – but I think she is telling me she works here.' Maria gulps. 'And now Sofia is stealing, even from her own sister! It is not like her…'

Her voice fades out and I'm thinking this is one solid sistery-mystery and I ain't got a *clue* what to *do*! But I'm not giving Maria more *stress*, that ain't the thing for me to con-*fess*.

'Give me a minute to think, yeah?'

My brain is spinning and I have to stand up.

Besides, my *bum* is *numb* – rapstars don't sit still for long. They like to walk the *street*, get with the *beat*. I start tapping the litter bins with an old plastic spoon I find on the floor. Check out that riddum, man!

It gets my mind on the *move* and now my body needs to *groove*. I jump onto a wall and start shakin' it all up…

'Wassup, Celebrity News Viewers! Today we're going underground, checking out the set of Rapstar J.B.'s latest promo video, Urban Trash.'

(Cut to video of Rapstar J.B. in baggy jeans, baggy tee, bracelets and bandana. He's standing on the roof of a black Mercedes, making with the hand-moves, shooting his mouth off and giving it all that.)

'He's tough. He's hard. He's an urban warrior…'

(Suddenly the Merc's tinted automatic window lowers. Cue: SFX – clouds of cigar smoke and the sound of harsh coughing.

The door opens and out steps a large,

cigar-smoking figure in dark glasses. It's Mr
Bling – the dodgiest, down-and-dirty rapper in town.
  Rapstar J.B. sniffs the air from up on the car's
roof...)

> *'Yo, Mr Bling, don't take this too personal*
> *You stink like an ash-tray / your bad breath is*
>   *worse an'all!*
> *I ain't staying to see you choke on that smoke*
> *I'm outta here 'fore you lay down an' croak!'*

(J.B. jumps up and spins right off the roof of the
shiny Mercedes and straight into...)

'*Yeuch!*

'Jamie, are you OK?' Maria reaches out and
grabs my arm – I've just landed in a litter bin
and I'm knee deep in urban trash. I'm *sinking*, and
it's *stinking*!

'Someone's dumped a belt in here and it's
tangled around my leg,' I wail. 'There's no way
I'm touching it, it's covered in—'

'Please,' says Maria, stuffing a wad of tissues
into my hand, 'you must get it. It is my bag!'

CHAPTER 10

Break-Dancing

I decide to play it cool. No lolly wrappers, half-eaten burgers or used nappies are going to beat Rapstar J.B.

'Stand back, Maria. I'm going in!'

Holding my nose with one hand I dive in with the other. My fingers untangle the strap and then fasten onto something hard. It might be a bag, it might be...uurgh! Don't even think about it!

'Let me see!' Maria shouts as I pull it free.

She finds more paper tissues and wipes it clean.

'My *pasaporte*, it is still here!' she says as she looks inside. 'And my photos...and my money.' She looks confused. 'It is all here, nothing taken...*nada*.' She slumps against the wall and slides down into a sitting position.

I'm confused, too, but my natural rapper instinct for trouble makes me check out my surroundings. That's when I see a pile of cards dumped next to the litter bin.

'Yo Maria, these are those business cards your sister and her friend were giving out in the mall. They must have got fed up and dumped the rest.' I pick one up to take a look. It says,

---

La Luna 🌙

Café/Restaurant
It's out of this world!

Save yourself the plane fare!
Come and try real Spanish food
in the heart of Sheffield.

(Weekends before 6 pm — two for the price of one)

At first it doesn't mean much to me, but this rapstar has learned to check out the small print. And I see some sneaky little letters at the bottom of the card: Richard English Language Schools.™

I let out a low whistle. 'Richard English again! This man's creating a global business empire.

He's trying to take over the world – or South Yorkshire, at least.'

Maria looks where I'm pointing and starts to get excited. 'We must go to this café right now – *¡pronto!* – perhaps we find my sister! You know where it is?'

I turn over the card and show her the address. 'No worries, we can take a bus there.'

She gives me a super-size smile. 'Thank you, J.B., you are helping me so much.' Then she holds out her hand, and I pull her to her feet.

'Hey, what are friends for?' I say. And suddenly I mean it, because Maria's OK, you know? I might even scrap the 'Revenge Rap', and risk losing millions, for the sake of world peace. Rappers are human, after all. And don't think I didn't notice – she finally got my name right, at last!

Half an hour and a bus ride later we're outside La Luna café. It seems that Mr Bling has a real empire in this part of Sheffield. He owns a whole network of buildings. There's the café, which is quite new; across the road from that is

La Luna Nightclub plus a hotel, and next to that there's the Language School, of course.

Even now, I can see students going through the school door with notebooks in their hands. I'm speechless. School on a Saturday afternoon! This Richard English guy is obviously pure evil.

We walk into the café and grab a table. 'OK Maria,' I say, peering over the menu at her, 'take some advice from an expert. Just act casual. The important thing is not to draw attention to yourself, hang loose—'

But before I can finish giving Maria my tips for keeping cool, I see Richard English walk in behind her. At the same time she points over my shoulder and gives a sudden squeal. So I turn round to see Sofia, waiting on tables at the other end of the café!

Of course, Maria jumps up pronto, ready to say hello (or ¡hola! or whatever) – but a streetwise rapper always works out where it's at before he makes his move. The King o' Bling's got bad vibes and I think we need to check out this whole sistery-mystery thing first. I have to distract Maria before she launches into a

South American kissing extravaganza.

Luckily there's a bangin' beat playing and that gives me an ide-*a*. My nerves disappe-*ar*, my mind goes cle-*ar*, I have no fe-*ar*...

'Hey, Maria! Check these moves, pay *attention*! I got more style than...a hair *extension*!' I yell out, then I'm standing up and moving to the music! She turns around...but only for a second – then she turns back again and heads towards her sister.

'And check this!' I do a moonwalk and people start clapping, but Maria ain't stopping.

'And what about this?' I do a back flip, then sit on the floor, clutch my knees and finish with a supercool tail-spin – round and round, like a turntable. I can see the two sisters' faces flashing by – Maria, Sofia, Maria, Sofia, Maria, Sofia.

Everyone's clapping and I'm getting faster and faster. This is my moment of glory. They're all impressed – well, I *am* a natural...

'Welcome back from the break, viewers. And now for our Famous Lives Bio-pic series.

'In today's show, we have a recording of Rapstar

75

J.B.'s famous turbo-powered tail-spin – his legendary trademark move – caught on camera.

'See J.B. step up the pace, he's faster than a cop-car chase! This is the move that shot him to fame, made his name and changed the course of rapstar his-tor-y.

'A word of warning though, to any kids tuning in right now: Don't try this at home, it'll end in—'

CCCcccccrrrrraaaaasssssbbbbbbbbb!!!!!

OK, so now I know why it's called break-dancing. That's the sound of half a dozen glasses smashing into tiny pieces as I bash into Sofia and her tray, sending them flying.

Before Maria can rush to help Sofia and spoil my distraction technique, I scramble to my feet then pretend to trip up again. This time I grab at Maria as I fall, pushing her away from her sister.

Everyone starts whooping and clapping and ...laughing. I'm not sure they're giving me the respect a rapstar truly deserves.

Then someone shouts, 'Better than the telly!' Hmmm, on second thoughts, perhaps I'll autograph a napkin or two.

Whump!

Suddenly I feel myself being lifted to my feet by the back of my T-shirt. Someone wants to speak to me and I don't think it's a talent scout.

I look up to find the icy-blue eyes of Richard English fixed on my face.

CHAPTER 11
Freestyle

'Now then, what's all this? A free floor show?' says Mr Bling in a voice as loud as a boom box and as fake as his tan.

'Sorry man, it's er...the cool music – gave me the *itch* to *twitch*,' I say, trying to wriggle free. 'Can I check on my friend here?'

'Yeah, 'course you can, son,' he shouts, aware that people are still listening in. But he turns down the volume for the next bit and growls, 'And I'll see you both in my office *now*, all right?'

He lets go of my collar and I pull Maria to her feet. 'Are you OK?'

'Yes I—'

'Sorry, Sir. Sorry, Miss,' Sofia interrupts. She keeps her eyes down as she bends to pick up some pieces of glass at our feet and clinks them onto her tray. She's showing no sign of knowing her sister.

Maria looks surprised but the fall must have knocked some sense into her because she keeps her lips zipped.

Then Sofia speaks again and her voice is high and nervous: '*Lo siento* – so sorry, Señor English, it is my fault, all my fault. I didn't see—'

Mr Bling opens his mouth, takes out his cigar and he's speaking, but I can't understand a word. Not that I need to – a rapper knows when something bad is goin' down and his tone is as sharp as a broken bottle. Sofia nods, and crouches as if she's been hit. She keeps her eyes lowered and continues to clear up the mess.

He clamps his cigar back in his mouth and fixes us with a *follow-me* look.

Richard English's 'office' is a tobacco-flavoured cupboard, with a table, chair and ashtray overflowing with cigar butts. It's not up to this rapstar's usual classy-club standard!

On the wall there's a massive glossy poster. It says:

The Richard English World-Wide Language Schools

No matter where you are,
we've got you covered!

Is that a promise or a threat? I wonder. Under the words on the poster there's a photo of a smiling Richard English – same streak-blond hair, orange tan and gold overload, but something's not quite right. Either this photo was taken thirty years ago or it's been air-brushed and digitally enhanced to a level that any superstar would die for.

'Is that *you?*' I ask in amazement. Rappers are like that, they just spit it out.

Maria shoots me a look but luckily, Mr English takes my remark as a compliment.

'Like father, like son,' he growls. 'You'd be surprised 'ow many people make that mistake. 'Course, Richard English Junior had all the advantages money can buy with a self-made man like me as his dad.'

'So you've got these language schools all over the world, have you?' I ask quickly. This is our chance to find out more about his shady set-up.

'Well, er...no. We've just got the one in Sheffield so far. I'm Director of UK Operations, so I'm in charge here. Junior does all the travelling – he's touring South America right now, recruiting kids for our courses. As this takes off, we're planning to open more UK schools and he'll tour more countries. There's big money to be made in learning English.'

So, why is Sofia's course so cheap? Where's the money coming from to fund his empire? His words just don't add up.

Mr Bling sits down at his desk, blows a smoke-ring in the air and snaps, 'OK, enough. Your turn to chatter, natter, patter and it better be good. What were you playing at out there?'

It's down to me – Maria still looks in a state of shock. But what can I say?

I open my mouth and...nothing comes out. A rapstar's worst nightmare. I'm choked. Literally.

I can't stop coughing because of all the smoke in the office. So I open a window and breathe deep.

Mr English leans towards me – up-close and far too personal. 'Make it quick or I'll—'

Suddenly Maria wheels around and her eyes flash. Her hair's gone electric again and I can see she's in rapper mode. She starts shooting her mouth off…

'Stop and look, please, into my eyes
You know that we came here for a surprise
We love to rap and we love to dance
So don't throw us out, just give us a chance.'

Mr Bling isn't impressed. He picks up the phone and Maria stops in mid-flow. I'm guessing she's worried he might bring the heavy mob in. I clocked some of those waiters earlier and they were no pushovers.

OK, so now the diva's down, Rapstar J.B. will show her how it's *really* done...

'Yo, Mr English! Her words are true
No word of a lie, er…no pile of poo
That's why we knocked down a glass or two
We were in such a rush to rap for you!'

He looks stunned – it's my natural talent, it has that effect on people. Even Maria is shaking her head in disbelief! Then she opens her mouth for the big finish...

'So we want to sign up, on the dotted line
For your Freedom Slam! – if you'll give us the
time?'

It works! Mr Bling slowly puts down the phone and asks for our names and what school we go to. Then he pulls out a piece of paper from a drawer and suddenly he's all smiles. He says our teachers have already put us forward for the Freedom Slam! (Don't I know it? Now there's no backing out.)

He takes us back out into the café and even orders us some free drinks – *on da house.*

As soon as he leaves, Maria smiles at me. *'Muchas gracias* again, J.B. I think we can work well as...a crew, don't you?' Then she raises her glass of orange juice to mine...

'Yo! It's Celebrity Update and we're here tonight with a world exclusive! Rapstar J.B. and Maria X. have stunned the rap world by announcing that they are going to rap together, as a crew. From now on they'll be known as JBX!

'Rapstar J.B. spoke to reporters earlier today and this is what he said:

"It's kinda strange that a good-looking, multi-talented solo rapstar like me is a forming a crew...but it's all good. Maria's a feisty female who shows some promise, so I've decided to help her out, that's all. She needs my rapping talent!

"And to all my female fans out there, I'm still at liberty, y'get me? This ain't no love-thing, call it a business move. Rapstar J.B.'s still free to get in the groove."

'And I've just heard that we're going over live to see the signing of the new deal. Yes, Maria X. is taking up the pen and...she signs. Now she's leaning forward and holding out the contract to Rapstar J.B. Wait a minute. Is she whispering sweet nuthin's in his ear...?'

'J.B. J.B., you must choose something from this menu...'

I take the menu Maria is holding out to me.

'So we can stay longer and I can talk to my sister,' Maria continues, still in a whisper.

'No worries, I'm always ready to eat,' I say, taking it off her and scanning the page. Then I lower my voice, 'But take a look at Mr *Bling*, doin' his *thing*.' He's playing the big MC in his flashy white suit, shouting orders and chatting to the customers. 'How are you going to talk to Sofia without him seeing you?''

Maria doesn't blink, she doesn't miss a beat. She looks me straight in the eye and shoots, 'You will find a way, J.B. I know it.'

CHAPTER 12
Big Noise

'OK, so there's something goin' down with your sister, but we don't know what deal Mr Bling is working,' I say, trying to skim-read the menu at the same time.

'He spoke to my sister in Spanish,' Maria whispers, her large dark eyes on mine. 'Very bad Spanish,' she adds, but this is no joke. She's serious.

'Yeah?' Of course, I'm interested, but my belly's in *da mood* for *food* right now and it's ready to rumble. 'What did he say?'

'He said Sofia must be more careful because she owes him so much money. He said she'd have to work even harder to pay it all back…she looked so scared.'

'But we knew she had to work to pay him for the school's English course, so what's new?' I'm staring at the menu but it's all in Spanish. 'Do you think they do chips?'

'J.B., Sofia came here for five hundred dollars but he says she owes him much more than that.'

I lower the menu. 'How much?'

Maria's voice is almost a whisper. 'Five thousand dollars. It's not true!'

That's big money, even for a *propa'* rapstar like me. Suddenly I'm not hungry – but we order some burgers just to buy extra time.

Maria is desperate to talk to Sofia but she's been avoiding our table like we're B-list celebrities at an A-list party. Why?

'What we need is a distraction to get Mr English off Sofia's back so you two can catch up,' I say eventually, thinking aloud.

Suddenly Maria reaches down for her bag and rummages around in it. She pulls out some grey, papery things – they look like sweets that are *way* past their sell-by date – and presses them into my hands.

'Brazilian fireworks,' she hisses. 'We use them for birthday parties, and I carry them for security too.'

'Security?'

'If you are alone and someone follows you

home, just throw them on the floor, hard. *Oop–a!* They make a *big* noise.'

'But, don't you need matches or something?'

She shakes her head and smiles. 'No, nothing.'

'Nuff said.' I'm outta that La Luna café and round the back of the kitchens faster than it takes to say *distraction*!

'Yo, and now for a bangin' Brazilian Beat to bring my show to a close. So, from Rapstar J.B. a BIG thank you to Hollywood, Paris and Grimly UK!

'And to all the fans in the audience and watching at home, dis is a Public Announcement! You have been WARNED! Listen-up for some x-tra boombastic special FX! You ain't heard nothing yet...!'

Bang!

    Bang!

        Bang!

If the screams of panic are anything to go by then my special FX have made quite an impression. Those Brazilian Bangers sure make a BIG noise!

I am just about to head back to the café when I clock an open window to the left of the kitchen doors – the same window I opened in Mr Bling's office earlier.

Yo, rapstars never miss the *chance* for a dra-ma-tic *entrance* and I haul myself up and through the window faster than you can say, 'hip-hop heavy'!

There's no welcome committee to greet me on the other side but I ain't losin' sleep over it. I'm here to dig deep into Mr Bling's *bizness* and find out the *real deal.*

It's dark in the office but I can make out Mr Bling's desk by the light from the yard outside. There's still lots of noise going on behind the office door that leads back through to the café and I figure I've got a few minutes (max) to *case da space.* Countdown.

I start pulling out drawers from the desk and rifling through papers but I have no idea what I'm looking for. All the time, my heart is banging like a beat box. What if someone finds me here? But Rapstar *J.B.* ain't about to *flee*, so I keep going.

In the bottom drawer I find a folder which I pull out and take over to the window. I hold it up to the light outside and some thin, red notebooks fall out onto the floor. When I pick them up I see gold lettering and patterns on the front – they're not notebooks...they're passports.

There must be at least twenty of them. I open one up and there's the face of our waiter in the Café Luna staring out at me. *Federico José Rodriguez*. I open another and another – they're all Spanish names and they are all about Sofia's age. The last one I check is Sofia's. I cram the passports back into the folder and ram them into the drawer to cover my tracks.

But why has Mr Bling got all their passports in a drawer in his office? There's still plenty of noise from the café, so I take a rapstar-risk and try the office-door handle. Locked. And something tells me only Richard English has the key. No one's getting their passport back without his say so.

But now's the time to quit the scene of the crime, pronto – if anyone saw that door handle move they might report it to Mr Bling. I drop back out of the window and head back inside.

I'm shakin' like a rapper with first-night stage fright but I tell myself to chill out, not freak out, 'cos Maria needs to know what I've found...

It's easy to blend in back at the café 'cos it's as mad as midnight in a city club. People are crowding round the kitchen like groupies round a guest star, trying to see *whass 'appenin'*.

Except, of course, for Maria and Sofia. They are standing behind a plastic palm tree, giving it some serious chat.

I move over to them, hoping to catch what they're saying. No chance – it's all in Spanish, but I clock the look on Sofia's face and her tears tell their own story. You don't need words to see when someone's *bleep*-scared! (Expletive deleted.)

Suddenly I can see the crowd round the kitchen's starting to break up, so I grab Maria by the arm and hiss, 'Party's over, time to go.'

Sofia gives Maria one last sad look, then she rushes off. She starts putting chairs straight and collecting dirty glasses while we shimmy back to our table.

Mr Bling emerges from the café kitchen

looking three shades more orange than usual. He flashes his smile like a paparazzi camera and announces: 'No worries, ladies and gents. Security check's over – it was just some kid's prank, that's all. So, now you can relax and get back to having a good time…'

Someone pumps up the volume on the stereo and drowns him out. Then he's deep in conversation with his staff, but I don't think we should outstay our welcome. As I dig into my pockets for some cash I see him looking our way. And he ain't happy!

'Come on, Maria, we're outta here,' I mutter, slamming some coins on the table.

Then we shoot off like fireworks into the night.

CHAPTER 13

Get Real

We don't stop running till we reach the bus station. Luckily the 137 to Grimly is in, so we collapse onto the back seat, gasping and wheezing like we only have seconds to live.

As the bus speeds through the night I finally catch my breath. 'So what did Sofia say?'

'Oh J.B., it is terrible. My sister owes the Richard English School too much money, more than she thought! He said she read the Earn as You Learn papers all wrong. She did not see the…you know, little words?'

'Small print. Why, what was in it?'

'Something about a *big* deposit my family must pay. But how? Sofia knows we cannot afford it and she did not want to worry us. So she works in the café or club and cleans in the hotel – long hours every day. She is so unhappy! She has no time to study. And she is not the only one in trouble. There are others like her.'

The other passports, I think to myself.

'None of them remember this small print Mr English speaks of,' Maria goes on. 'But he insists. So when they are sent to the mall to give out business cards, they sometimes steal too…to pay back the money, they owe so much. Señor English even knows this, Sofia says.'

'So she stole your bag for the money? But she didn't take it…'

'No, she did not know it was mine, so when she saw my *pasaporte…¡que sorpresa!* She panicked and threw it away.'

'Maria, does this happen to all the students studying at the language school?'

'No. Sofia says some students, they pay a lot of money and they come to study all day, like at a proper school. Only the Earn as You Learn students are told they owe a lot of money.'

'Yeah and they're the ones who couldn't afford to pay much in the first place, who'll do anything not to worry their families, hundreds of miles away. This is one sharp operation – pick on the weakest ones who won't fight back,' I snarl. 'It's criminal! It's a con. And it's…slave labour. Why don't they go to the police? We could—'

'No! Richard English Junior, he knows my country. He came to my town. He knows people there…Sofia heard that your family will be hurt if you do not pay. That is why she didn't want to speak to me at the café. We must *not* go to the police.'

'OK, what if we warn your family and then help Sofia escape and go back to South America—'

Maria shakes her head sadly. 'No, my sister is not free. Mr English has taken her *pasaporte* and he won't give it back until she pays him the money. She cannot go home now, without her *pasaporte* she is an illegal. A nothing. And if she goes to the police, without ID? Well, she is a thief, no? They will arrest her anyway…'

A tear trickles down Maria's face, but she brushes it away fiercely and glares out of the window.

For once this rapper doesn't know what to

say, but my mind is on rewind. Five minutes ago I had Sofia's passport in my hand. But I don't think Maria can take any more – so I decide not to tell her. I close my eyes and I can still see the photos and names of all the other people in the passports. Each has a story to tell, like Sofia. But they can't speak up. Richard English said learning a language sets you free but he lied. He's tied a gag around Sofia's mouth and done the same to all the other students like her.

Now I want to say, *Whoa!* Show's over. This ain't going to *plan, man*. I want stretch limos, lights and fame, not someone else's pain. But Maria's all alone in a strange country, like a gatecrasher at a party, and she needs me. It's time to switch off the bright lights, come down off the stage and get real.

I'll start by finding out more about Maria and her life. 'If you and your sister both want to learn English so much, does that mean you want to come and live here?'

Maria tries to smile. 'Oh no, I love my country. I will never leave it. We have had our troubles but things get better, little by little. Today, many people need English for their work or they need to study in another country. I want to study law – it is my dream. I hope to study in England or America for a while. But then I will come home again, to work. I will be a human rights lawyer and fight to make things better still. For justice, but no violence.' She smiles properly now. 'I heard this in a rap song, you know it?... "Words are My Weapons"'

'Too right – a rapstar's anthem. Respect,' I say, and hold up my hand.

Maria gives me a high five and smiles. 'J.B., I am glad we met,' she murmurs. 'I told my sister you will help her. You will know what to do next.'

Touching Maria's skin makes me tingle – like she's running her own electric current and I've just plugged in. We suddenly seem so in tune with each other, so in harmony...

'Yo! This is an x-tra special night, party people! The first gig for the new rap crew, HARMONY JBX!

'As you know, chart-topping Rapstar J.B. has joined up with South American singing sensation Maria X – and we're guessing this combo will be hotter than a chilli-pepper taco with x-tra-hot sauce!

'So, now over to the opening of the show and a rap penned by J.B. himself:'

(Darkness; on one side of the stage a spotlight pinpoints a single rapstar and his mic.)

J.B.: People all over the world, ain't you had enuff? Chattin' and cussin' and all that kind of stuff?

(On the other side of the stage a second spotlight pinpoints a single girl-rapper and her mic.)

M.X.: And crying and lying but the question is this: Why waste your breath when you can use it for a...kiss?

(The two rappers move across the stage to face each other.)

J.B. and M.X. (vocals in harmony): Why waste your breath when you can use it for a kiss?
Why waste your breath when you can use it for a...

Suddenly my lips are on Maria's and it's no publicity stunt. It's not a celebrity air-kiss either.

This is the *real deal.*

CHAPTER 14
Big Time

Someone presses the stop button and time stands still.

Then the bus driver shouts, 'Grimly Bus Station. Everybody off!' and I realise it's not time, but the bus that is standing still.

Maria and I pull apart in embarrassment and stumble down the steps without looking at each other. We don't speak; what is there to say? Only our footsteps echo like a backbeat on the empty streets as we walk home. When Maria said I would know what to do next, I don't think kissing was what either of us had in mind!

I don't see much of Maria on Sunday. I'm grounded for bringing her home late and she has to go out and meet some other exchange students. So I'm stuck in my room alone, wondering what we can do for her sister. I even flick through some local papers and listen to the radio news. I'm facing up to reality now and it's quite a surprise. You know, there's a whole new world out there beyond celebrity-land!

When it all gets too much I put on some music, think about Maria and scribble words on my hands...then I wash them all off again in case people think I've gone soft – I can't disappoint my fans!

Next morning, Big Mo drives us to school. I want to talk with Maria but it's hardly the time to have a heart-to-heart with your honey when your driver's eyeballing you in the rear-view mirror.

It's only at lunchtime that I get the chance to speak with her properly. We're standing in line and there are some words on the tip of my tongue that taste worse than school dinners.

'Maria, I've been thinking...this is big time! Mr Bling is acting like some sort of *Gangmasta*, isn't he? He's all over the *Sheffield Weekly News* – building a *bizness* empire. And after Saturday, we know where he gets the money and the workers from – it's not Earn as You Learn; more like Work All Day for Zero Pay! We have to go to the police—'

I might as well have pressed a repeat button. Her reaction is exactly the same as before. '*Police? Never!* It is too risky. I *told* you yesterday. In my country we sort our own troubles. There was a time we couldn't trust the police... *We* will find a way to save Sofia.'

'But how? This is one shady set-up! What can we fight it with?'

Sofia juts out her jaw. The diva is back! 'Words are our weapons, J.B. Remember, the Freedom Slam! is tomorrow night at the English School. We must do something then.'

I'm getting angry now and hungry, too – not a good mix. Mrs Burns, the lunchtime supervisor, is waiting for me to choose some food but I have to give Maria a mouthful first.

'So what are we gonna do at the Freedom Slam!? *Lash 'im wid our lyrics? Ram 'im wid our rhymes?* You don't think—'

'Promise me you will not go to the police.'

'I—'

She grips my arm and her knuckles are white. 'Promise!'

'OK. Don't stress, I promise! But you are so pig-headed!'

'No pigs' heads on the menu today luv,' says Mrs Burns. 'You want to choose something else, instead?'

'So you are calling me a pig?' Maria hisses. 'You *burro estúpido.*'

'Now then, young lady, I have visited my sister in Spain every summer for the last twenty years and I know what that means,' Mrs Burns says crossly. 'There are no stupid donkeys on the menu today, either.'

No hip-hop heavy can take that sort of chat without hitting back! I look round for inspiration. 'Yeah, enough of the Spanish insults – try a Yorkshire one, loony-spoon!'

'I beg your pardon, young man!' Mrs Burns is overheating now.

'*Idiota!*' Maria explodes.

'And who are you calling an idiot?' Mrs Burns snaps. 'That's enough from both of you!'

But Rapstar J.B.'s got to have the last word.

'Just leave it, Maria, you…manky muppet!'

'OK. That's it—'

In the end, it's Mrs Burns who has the last word, and it's, 'OUT!'

So we miss our lunch and I drift through the rest of the day in a hunger-daze. No one seems to notice the difference…

Mr Turner keeps us back after school, 'just to talk, discuss, have meaningful dialogue,' as he puts it. Maria and I sit at desks on opposite sides of the room because talking is the last thing *we* want to do, but Mr Turner doesn't notice. He bounces round the room in excitement.

'So, are you ready for tomorrow night – the event, the happening, the Freedom Slam!?'

His cheerful smile fades out when Maria and I stare blankly back at him, our faces fixed in freeze-frame.

'Oh dear, a case of stage-fright, methinks,' he continues. 'Never mind, perhaps if we enter you together? I could call Richard English to explain…then you can practise at home and support each other as a couple, a pair, *a crew—*'

'Never!'

'No chance!'

Mr Turner blinks in surprise at this outburst.

'Ah, I see. Well, I suppose it's a case of er...'

'Serious artistic differences,' I say.

'Yes, *he* can't rap!' Maria snaps.

'Oh, that's *so* cutting! Is my blood on the carpet?'

'Please!' Mr Turner interrupts. 'Save all that er...verbal energy for the Slam!, the contest, the battle.'

Suddenly it all seems pointless. Can you believe it? Yesterday we were *kissin'* – today we're *dissin'*. Now I'm as mixed up as a mega-remix-album.

Is Maria really the same girl I felt so in tune with last night?

CHAPTER 15
Gangmasta Flash

Maria and I end up walking out of the school gates at the same time but definitely not together, if you know what I mean.

As we hit the main street, Maria picks up speed, head down, trying to get away from me. So she doesn't see a black Mercedes cruise after us, slow and sinister like a circling shark. It's not the typical set of wheels you see in the Grimly 'hood.

The car picks up speed and then stops on the corner ahead, where we cross the road to get home. Maria still doesn't notice, so I break into a run and catch up with her. OK, we both have our pride but this is no time to play the solo artist.

We draw level with the Merc and the tinted window slowly rolls down to reveal a cigar and a blaze of bling. Gangmasta Flash himself, aka

Richard English, as large as life and twice as ugly.

There's a puff of smoke and then his gruff voice. 'Word of advice, kids, fireworks are for grown-ups,' he says, leaning towards the open window. 'Don't mess with the big boys, OK?'

I guess he wasn't impressed by the Brazilian bangers. But has he worked out about my office visit, too? There's more to come. 'Now, hold out your hand. I gotta little present for ya,' Mr English growls.

Maria whispers, '*Non!*' in my ear but I don't have much choice. Mr Bling has a muscle-man driver and this could turn nasty. Maria might think words are weapons, but I'm not about to put them to the test.

I cup open my palm and he puts something in it. A photo, I think. Then he taps his cigar and drops hot ash on it before folding his other leather-gloved hand around my own and squeezing it. He's forcing me to mash-up the photo *good and propa* and I bite my lip as the heat prickles my palm.

'See you tomorrow night then, kids,' he says.

'It's all good publicity for us, so we don't want anything to go wrong, do we? Best behaviour, don't forget, or you might live to regret it.' Then he lets go of my hand. The tinted window rolls back up and the car glides away.

As soon as the Merc is out of sight, Maria takes my hand and cradles it gently. It's almost worth the pain, just for this!

As the feeling comes back into my crushed fingers, I unbend them, take out the screwed-up photo and shake off the ash. When it's spread out on a nearby wall I can't believe what I'm seeing.

It's a picture of my Big Mo going into her salon, Curl Up and Dye. I always said that was a bad name for a hairdresser's – now it seems positively evil. My stomach lurches like an elevator and I feel like someone just punched me in the gut. Is Richard English threatening my m—

Suddenly a car screeches to a halt in front of us and before I can look up a deep, booming voice orders, 'Get in the car, both of you, NOW!'

I've never been so happy to see Big Mo – aka

my mum – in my entire life.

She ain't happy though, she's mad at me for being late home from school. She's getting paranoid after our extended weekend shopping trip and she doesn't even know *da truth* about what's really going down.

We drive home in silence as rain starts to fall outside, and all I can hear is the sad sound of the windscreen wipers,

Swisssh swish! *Swisssh* swish! *Swisssh* swish!

It's a good beat...

Rapstar J.B. is in a mellow mood today. He's working on a rap ballad as a tribute to his family...

'Back when you were young / only Mom would do
If you fell down or got scared or caught the flu
But then you grew older / felt bolder / and you told her!

'So now you're the boss, going about your own bizness
But you can't forget your Momma – hey! I'm serious!

There's only ONE Momma not, two, three or four,
Only one momma, you ain't got any—'

Stop! Rewind! Delete. What happened to getting real? It's hard to kick the raps to riches lifestyle – but I look at the raindrops trickling down the glass and the world is blurred and changed.

This is what it's like for Maria. Her sister – her whole family – is in trouble and she's scared. So are all those other students. Mr Bling needs to be stopped and J.B. has to help do it. I promised not to go to the police and a rapper's word is his...well, *word.* If he hasn't got that, he's got nothing. And Maria knows it. So I'll have to think of another *plan.* Something at da Freedom *Slam!* to get us out of this big *jam.*

I've got to get over our 'artistic differences' and help Maria, Sofia and the other students. It's time to take the rap for real!

CHAPTER 16

Shake Your Booty

When we get home I'm put straight under bedroom-curfew orders for being late back from school. Big Mo doesn't include Maria in this but she's got that don't-mess-wid-me look on her face, so I don't argue back. Besides, she's a loyal member of staff and it just shows she cares!

In my room I can't stop thinking about the other night on the bus with Maria. 'Words are our weapons,' she said. She really believes it and maybe she's *right*. Is there more to rapping than just making money? It's time to put up a fight and find out. J.B. needs to spit the truth about what's really going down at the Richard English School. OK, not to the police…but Maria didn't make me promise not to go to the press…

Yes, ex*press* it, don't *stress* it – that's *da plan, man*! This Slam! is all about advertising the

school, so local press will be there. Free
publicity, *innit?* I stand up and chat to the
mirror. I'm on a roll now and my ideas flow
with style…

'Yo, this is the deal
First up I go all out to win the Slam!
Let's face it, who else? I'm your man!
'Cos everyone loves a winner, it's true
When you're Number One they listen to
you
So the press wants an interview after
the show
And I dish the dirt on Mr Bling, so they're
in the know!
It'll be a front page they'll never forget
The biggest thing to happen since I was
born, you bet!
The law moves in when it reads the goss
To show Mr Bling (and son) just who is
da boss!'

Hmm, I'm guessing Maria will be pret-ty
grateful when my plan works out…and I won't

say no to the extra publicity, either. Yo, live the dream!

As everything depends on me winning the Slam! it's time to work on the image, 'cos if a rapper looks the part, he'll be the part. This is one serious dress rehearsal.

I find my baggiest jeans and put them on, followed by my biggest trainers. I undo the laces and pull out the tongues to make them look even more cool, but when I try walking my feet keep slipping out of them. Hmmm. Not so much Snoop Dogg as Slip-Slopp. No worries, I'll sort it later.

Next up, the white T-shirt. OK, so it's not x-tra tight and designed to show off my muscles but, hey!, pushing a pen all day at school doesn't exactly build up your biceps.

Now let's focus on the headgear. I tie on a big white bandana (well, it's Big Mo's headscarf that she uses at the salon. Don't think the fans will notice – as long as they don't storm the stage).

I check out the look in my bedroom mirror but it's too small for me to see the full-body effect. Big Mo and Maria are watching TV downstairs, so I sneak into Mo's bedroom.

I click the door shut and switch on the radio, moving the tuner until I find some raps. There's a full-length mirror in here and it's time to practise some moves. I start with some mean and moody poses with my hands in cool rapper mode. Check it, dude!

But there's still something missing. Yeah, a definite lack of bling. I rootle around in Big Mo's jewellery box and find a big gold locket and jangly charm bracelet. Sorted.

The rap music's stepping up a beat now so I try a few shimmies and start shakin' my booty like there's no tomorrow. Yo!

Then I stop.

Suddenly.

Isn't shimmying and shaking strictly for the girls? I don't know. *Hmmm.*

In the end I decide to stand very still, deliver the rap straight and use limited hand moves *only.* You can never be too careful – years of street cred could be wiped out in seconds by shaking the wrong body part.

Finally the rap itself. No worries, there. I've already scribbled a few notes down. I'm calling it my 'Big-Up-Yourself Get-Outta-Grimly Freedom Rap'. Catchy title – kinda trips off the tongue. Some of the rhymes aren't quite right yet but I'll fix them as I go along.

I grab the hairbrush like a mic. Check it out!

'See ya, Grimly, I'm heading for the top
Don't stop me now, 'cos rap's all I got
I'm lean and mean like a...*tangerine?*
　　　　　　　er...*love machine?*
　　　　　　　er...*rap magazine?* Yo!
I'm lean and mean like a rap magazine
The best there is – gonna live the dream!

My name's Rapstar J.B. – yes, I'm the
　　best
And one day soon I'll...have hairs on my
　　chest—'

Just then the door bursts open and Big Mo appears in the bedroom with Maria right behind her. I stop mid-rap, arms wide, and catch sight of myself freeze-framed in the full-length mirror. Not the best publicity shot ever.

'Jamie, what's all the noise?' Big Mo starts. 'And *why* are you wearing my headscarf?'

Doh! Why can't a trapdoor open up right now and drop me into celebrity-land where things like this *never* happen?!

Then she takes a step closer, eyeballing me real hard like a bouncer on red alert.

'And is that my charm bracelet you're wearing...and my necklace...?'

CHAPTER 17
Mixin' It

'Yo, Sheffield. Let me hear you shout, "Yeah"!'

'Yeah!'

'I can't hear you Sheffield. I said, "Yeah"!'

'YEAH!'

It's the Freedom Slam! for real now and I'm standing at the back of a packed Richard English School hall, between Maria and Big Mo. I'm looking pret-ty cool, even without the bandana and bling which were seized in last night's raid.

I've spent the whole day trying to get Maria on her own to let her know I'm taking care of things tonight but I'm sure she's been avoiding me. Probably thinks I'm going to bring up the police thing again.

The hall is jammed with kids from all the schools in the area, and the local press fills a whole row of seats at the back. If this doesn't bring in more Bling business, nothing will. Unless I can stop him!

Mr Bling himself is on stage, and he's trying to talk the talk in his gravelly voice.

'All-right. We're here tonight for the Freedom Poetry Slam! and we've even got a live satellite video link up to my son, Richard English Junior, from his tour of South America!'

There's a screen hanging down at the side of the stage and suddenly it flashes on, showing a younger, slimmer, even-more-orange Mr Mini-Bling, with some waving teenagers.

'Now, we want to give you local kids the chance to show off your talent tonight and, of course, to big-up the Richard English Language School!'

'Raaah!' Cheers from a group of Richard English's students sitting near the front. I wonder how many of them are 'real' language students and how many are on the same Work-All-Day-for-Zero-Pay deal as Sofia?

'So this is how it works. Each competitor performs their rap and then we'll ask *you* out there to be the judges. *You* make the noise and, depending on how loud it is, my assistants here will hold up three score cards.'

The assistants file on stage. One of them is Sofia and I recognise the other two as workers from La Luna café. They all look nervous and Sofia's eyes are darting everywhere till she spots Maria. Then her eyes widen – I'm not sure if it's with fear or hope, but either way it makes me more determined to win this for the girls in my life and the folks in my 'hood! I'm in such a great mood I squeeze Maria's arm and whisper, 'Good luck!'

She turns and gives me a tiny smile which starts my heart skipping like a snare-drum.

'Oh, J.B. I am so preoccupated, I am not incentivated!' she whispers and I know her well enough by now to understand that she's worried about her sister and can't pump herself up for the Slam!

Before I can set her straight and tell her about the J.B. rap-plan which will see Mr Bling face the music, she's up off of her chair and running out of the hall.

'Oh, Jamie. What have you done now?' Big

Mo wags a finger at me. Huh, whatever happened to staff loyalty?

'What? How was that my fault?'

'Never mind, just go and find her – the competition is about to start... Unless you want me to take her place on stage? Do you think your friends will be impressed when I strut my stuff?'

I jump up extra-fast and head for the exit.

In the corridor just outside I hesitate. Will Big Mo – aka my one and only mum – be safe in there alone? But Richard English can't do much to her while she's in a crowd and it's Maria I need to worry about now. I have to find her fast.

Luckily she's in the first place I look – sobbing her heart out among the coats in the cloakroom. The *caring, sharing* role doesn't come naturally to a hardman like *me*, Rapstar J.*B.*, but I sit down next to her and even try some shoulder patting. 'Hey, Maria. Look...it's all good. Don't get upset. I have a pla—'

Suddenly she blows her nose super-loud and wails, 'I can't do my rap, J.B. I'm scared.

It's impossible!'

'What?'

'My rap – it's crap-rap, like yours, you know?'

For once I ignore her insult because I'm so surprised by what lies beneath it. Maria – who always seems so brave, so confident, so sure of herself – Maria has stage fright?

'No way, Maria. You're brilliant! You're the best rapper I've heard.'

And as soon as I say it, I know it's true, though I'll sue anyone else who says so.

'But this rap is very important – *¡muy inportante!*' she sobs. 'It is my plan to save Sofia and I don't know if it is so good…'

So Maria's got a plan too? 'Have you got your rap written down?' I ask now. 'D'you want me to check it out?'

She hands me a piece of paper – her rap.

I'm stunned. OK, so 'words are our weapons' – but Maria's really loaded them up tonight. I read them over and over. If she shoots off this rap and people hear what she's saying, it's gonna bring da house down!

At least I hope so, 'cos for this to work

people don't just have to listen to what Maria's saying – they've got to join in and make their own words into weapons, too.

If they don't hear her loud and clear, she's running a big risk. She's disrespecting Mr Bling and he'll be out for revenge. And it won't just be Maria he'll be out to get. It'll be Sofia, too. And me – and my mum…It's gotta work!

Maria fixes me with big watery eyes. 'J.B., what shall I do?'

Compared to Maria's fighting talk, my own 'Big-Up-Yourself Get-Outta-Grimly Freedom Rap' suddenly looks like verbal candy – it melts on your tongue and disappears. But Maria's words stay with you 'cos they mean something, they're about putting yourself on the line for what's right – and isn't that the point?

'You go for it, Maria. That's what you do.'

She shakes her head. 'J.B., I'm scared. I can't do it on my own…'

She doesn't need to spell it out.

I hold out my hand to help her up.

'You're not on your own, Maria. We're in this together.'

CHAPTER 18

First Up

We take a few minutes to practise the rap and I even add some new lines, myself. Maria knows the words off by heart but I make notes on my hands. And arms, and right up to my elbow!

Then we go back to the main hall. Just as we are about to enter, I see a man wearing a press pass, scribbling away. Maria goes on ahead, but I hang back for a chat. First rule of stardom – never miss a chance to big-up yourself! Only for once, it's not me I'm talking about…

'What took you so long?' Big Mo's waiting for us just inside the hall. 'The show's nearly over – the Richard English School crew are on next and then it's you. I had to ask them to change the running order.'

'What's the top score so far?'

'9/9/10. A solo act from Sheffield. Good luck!'

I don't like leaving Big Mo on her own again but we don't have a choice. It's time to get up on stage and wait in the wings. This rap plan better work.

'OK, next up is a posse called Word Perfect,' Mr Bling announces. 'And what better advert for my school than these four students who study English with us. Give it up Sheffield – and our fans overseas – for Word Perfect!'

The crowd erupts and the live video-link pans out to show more screaming kids behind Richard English Junior. It's a safe bet that some of them will be the next victims of his dodgy Earn as You Learn scheme – unless we stop it.

Two girls and two boys run on stage...

'A – B – C – D
Freedom's for you and freedom's for me
E, F, G, H and I – J – K
English is the key and that's what we say
L, M, N – O, P, Q, R
Richard English is a star

S – T – U – V
Freedom's for you and freedom's for me
Don't forget W – X – Y – Zed
Take it from the top and repeat what I said!'

They are seriously sad. They are mega-moronic. But no one seems to notice and it's obvious why not. From our place in the wings, I can see Mr Bling's backstage crew throwing lotsa freebies out into the crowd: T-shirts, badges, tickets and vouchers.

Meanwhile, Word Perfect keep making beat-box noises, and asking the crowd to join in, until the whole room pulsates with the words...

'L, M, N – O, P, Q, R
Richard English is a star!'

At last the crew on stage stop rapping and bow their heads. There's a second of silence before the badge-wearing, voucher-waving crowd explodes, clapping and shouting.

Richard English struts back on stage. 'And the score is...'

One card goes up – 9.

Another card goes up – 10.

Now it's Sofia's card. She turns it over slowly – 9.

Even though that's exactly the same as the other top score, Mr Bling doesn't look too worried. It's obvious this competition is as fixed as his gelled-back hair!

He shouts into the mic. 'Yo, Sheffield! Remember that the audience is judging this too! What do you think of those 9s? Higher?'

And the crowd shouts back, 'HIGHER!' over and over – their voices rising like a diva's top note…

'HIGHER

HIGHER

HIGHER!'

Mr Bling knows how to work the crowd. I watch closely and see him wink at his on-screen son (Mini-Bling). Then he gives a quick nod to Sofia. Slowly, she puts down her number 9 scorecard and holds up…a number 10.

The crowd roars. Mr English grabs the mic again, 'And the final score is 9, 10, 10! How can you beat that?'

My thoughts exactly.

Then over the whoops and whistles Mr Bling starts talking again: 'But don't forget, it's not over yet!' The cheers change to boos and I hold my breath 'cos I know what's coming next.

'Now, now, be fair,' he growls, flashing a fake smile. 'Everyone deserves a chance. We still have two competitors left, both from Grimly High. We'll end with a young lady called Maria X, but first up is…Rapstar J.B.!'

'Yo! I said hello, London, New York, Tokyo and welcome to my global show. Dis is Rapstar J.B. an' we're beaming out world-wide! I can feel you all eye-ballin' me north, south, east and west-side…and I'm lovin' it—'

Reality check. I'm not lovin' it. I'm shaking like a shimmy and I'm sweating like a pig with sun-stroke. No joke. I can't afford to choke. I open my mouth and…hope.

'Yo, Sheffield. It's me, Rapstar J.B.….'

CHAPTER 19
Freedom Rap

'Yo, rapping is thinking and feeling
and more
It's praying what you're saying makes
some kinda sense
To at least one kid out in the audience...'

I pause...it feels so lonely on this stage. Then I turn and signal Maria to come over – we're in this thing together, after all. She takes the mic...

'We're thinkin' deep on what freedom
means to you and me
And how we can make rhymes that will set
us all free...'

Something is happening in the room. Maria's electric and the audience can't help tuning in. There's a stillness, they're waiting...and it's my turn again...

> 'Now I'd like to take a minute to have my
>   say
> 'Bout what freedom means to me here in
>   the UK
> Like wearing designer labels of every make
> So, abolish school uniform for freedom's
>   sake!'

'Y-e-a-h!' The audience starts cheering. They're really with us now. Let's give them something *serious* to think about...

> 'Time to listen-up to a sista MC
> Who's got her own ideas about living free
> Check it out – you're in for a massive
>   surprise
> Looking at life through someone else's
>   eyes.'

I hand the mic back to Maria and she *moves* to the *groove* again...

'Yo, flash designer labels – get outta here!
Freedom, to me, is living without fear
For your life, not just yours, but your
    family's too
'Cos freedom depends on your point of
    view.'

The crowd waits in silence, ready to catch what Maria says next. I wonder if Richard English has worked out where this is going? I try to check if Mum's OK but all I can see out front are bright lights.

Next to me, Maria takes a deep breath, opens her mouth and lets it flow...

'If you're working every day – that's 24/7
Then a chance to go to school would be
    like heaven
Abolish school uniform? That ain't so
    brave...
*When some kids out there are working like
    slaves!*

We both say the last line together. Maria's

pointing her finger accusingly towards Richard English and the judges, but before she can carry on Mr Bling takes control.

He's standing up making cutting moves across his neck. Is he threatening to slit our throats?

No, but he has got the sound to Maria's mic cut off!

Richard English's voice rumbles into his own mic. 'Listen-up, people! These Grimly High kids are cheating. They registered as solo artists. They can't rap as a crew. So they're out…'

He starts across the stage towards us. *Whass 'appenin, man? This wasn't in the plan!* If our words can't be heard we've lost our weapons. But before Mr Bling reaches us, loud boos from the audience stop him in his tracks. Then the chanting starts,

'Grim-ly

Grim-ly

GRIM-LY.'

Suddenly Sofia is on her feet and holding a scorecard high in the air – it's a 10!

But I know it took a lot of guts for her to do

that – what if the other judges aren't so brave? The second judge stands up, he's shaking...but he shows his scorecard – another 10! The third judge hesitates for a second then does the same. Three 10s – we've won!

And the strange thing is that it doesn't even matter. What matters more is that people heard what we said. They were all listening! And we have to let them hear the rest. But how?

The audience is yelling wildly for an encore and there's panic in Mr Bling's eyes. For the first time tonight he's lost control of the crowd. On the link-up screen, I can see Mini-Bling panicking, too.

Suddenly there's a high-pitched *Eeeeee!* Someone's put the sound back on! I grab the mic and my chance...

'Yo, let's take some time to big-up Maria
She's told us what it's like to live in fear
All of us here are united by one word
Time to shout it out loud so you can be
    heard...
Lemmee hear you say, FREEDOM!'

I hold the mic out to the audience and hear a faint echo, 'Freedom!'

It sounds pathetic. We've got to wind them up – ready for our big finish. 'Is that the best you can do? Check it out, FREEDOM!' I try again.

'FREEDOM!' – the echo comes back louder.

'One more time, FREEDOM!'

'FREEDOM!' The crowd shouts long and loud.

Now they're really on our side.

Time to kick ass. (Oops, sorry, is the mic still on? Can you cut that?)

CHAPTER 20

Name and Shame

I hold up my arms, until the room is totally silent. Only then do I start my *flow*, keepin' it deep and *low*...

> 'There's someone right here who stole
>   your names
> But it ain't for us to name and shame...'

I pass the mic to Maria who takes up where I left off...

> 'Speak up, if you've been conned and
>   threatened too,
> There's only one way out and it's down to
>   you.'

Maria turns to the judging panel. Sofia's eyes are wide with fright now and I guess Maria thinks maybe we've gone too far because she pauses and looks across at me.

For this to work, not only does the audience have to listen-up but the very people who have the most to lose have to speak up too. Only one Big Voice will shout down the Lords of the Blings. Unity is da key!

When your words are *right*, you'll win the *fight,* I tell myself. We've come this far and we can't stop now. I grab the mic again, keeping my voice strong and steady...

'You gotta shout out his name, long, loud
   and clear
Do it all together and beat the fear!'

And it's a wrap! Finito. The end. We've done all we can do, said all we can say, but is it enough to save us? I hold out the mic to the audience and put my other arm around Maria and we take a bow. There's a heartbeat of silence and then a *roar!* to rival any crowd at the Hollywood Bowl.

But this isn't the sound Maria and I are

waiting for. Have we got it wrong? Weren't they listening after all? In my head the words are stuck on repeat...

You gotta shout out his name, long, loud
and clear
Do it all together and beat the fear!

Mr Bling's starting to look his smug self again. He's reaching for his mic but I'm there first. 'Yo, make words your weapons!' I yell, using shock-jock tactics. One last try to make things happen.

Then we hear it. That one voice we were asking for – small but clear enough for us to pick it out,

'Rich-ard Eng-lish.'

It's Sofia, of course. She's naming and shaming him. Maria waves her over, along with the two other student judges, and they yell into the mic together,

'Rich-ard Eng-lish, RICH-ARD ENG-LISH'

And suddenly the name is coming from all directions. The students backstage are joining us up front, and some students in the audience are shouting out, too. They're all naming and shaming Richard English as the freedom-stealing fake that he is! Respect!

Things start happening in fast-forward then. Mini-Bling is already off the scene – there's only an empty chair left on the live link-up screen. The game's up for Mr Bling, too, but as he tries to make a break for it I'm way ahead of him. Like all good rapstars my moves are *fast*. I grab a fire extinguisher from the wings and *blast –*

Woooooossssssshhhh!

Richard English is covered in white foam. He starts skanking round the stage, slipping and sliding like a breakdancer on ice. Finally he does a brilliant back flip and falls smack on his butt.

A press camera starts popping and the audience cheers and calls out for more. Half of them still don't know exactly what's really going down but Mr Bling is *def* in disgrace. He doesn't get up for an encore, anyway. Though this might have something to do with a posse of bodyguards standing over him, made up of a few teachers, parents and Big Mo, of course. Glad she's OK...she'll get a bonus when we're done.

Meanwhile Maria and Sofia are reunited in their much longed-for South-American kissing extravaganza. They're laughing and crying and fast-talking in Spanish, all at the same time. Suddenly I feel really left out. Rapstars aren't usually lost for words...wish I could click a language switch in my head.

Then Maria turns to me, 'Oh, *perdón*, I am so sorry. I must present my sister to you. Sofi, this is J.B. He is the best rapper in *todo el mundo* – the whole world!'

Ain't it da truth! Sofia must agree 'cos now she starts kissing me instead of Maria... Hmmm, I could get used to this!

Finally, one of Sofia's student crew calls her over and at last I'm alone with Maria. She smiles. '*Muchas gracias*, Rapstar J.B. How can I ever thank you?'

There are times when actions speak louder than words and this is one of them. I lean in towards Maria and she leans in towards me. I close my eyes and—

'POLICE! Nobody move!'

CHAPTER 21

Words Matter

Three days later I smuggle Big Mo's laptop into my room so I can dial up the internet. The home page headline grabs my attention:

UK Freedom Poetry Slam!

Young Rapstars J.B. and Maria X Use Word Power to Trap Conmen!

ANDY MOLE REPORTS ONLINE

Richard English and Son arrested at home and abroad

Yo! You're going down, Mr Bling and Mini-Bling! It turns out they nailed Junior as he was leaving the studio after the Slam!. Great news – but I'll read the goss later.

Right now I need to check my inbox. Maria's staying with Sofia and the other students while the police check their stories and recover their passports – after a tip-off from me, nuff said. She promised to e-mail as soon as she could.

I haven't seen her since the Freedom Slam! and the house is empty without the other half of my crew. Quiet, too. I hope they'll let her come home soon so we can to celebrate our win and party rapstar style!

'Yowser! It's midnight at the party of the year, people! And it's time to put smiles, tears, hopes and fears in the mix, 'cos we're about to find out who's won the Solid-Gold Mesablaster-Motor-Mouth award for the best rapstar act of the year. Are you ready?

'First-up, let's look at the favourites to win this award.'

(Camera to table two.)

'Yo, it's JBX the hot new rap crew, featuring Rapstar J.B. and Maria X., in their matching diamond-studded bandanas.
  'These two look every inch the King and Queen of rap and they're dressed ready to par-tee. So, will they win?
  'And here to present the award are last year's winners, The Booty Crew!'

(Big Booty steps forward and speaks into the mic.)

'There are three nominees in this category but only one crew can win the award.'

(Li'l Booty hands him an envelope which Big Booty holds up high.)

'So, you want me to open it for you...?'

'Jamie, did you hear me? I said, I see you've got an e-mail from Maria. Are you going to open it? What does it say? Shall I open it?'

'Yo! Restricted access, Mum. And I didn't hear you knock...'

'Well, the door was open so—'

'Excuse me, Madam, I'll have to ask you to leave. This is a private club...'

As soon as she closes the door behind her I open the e-mail and start to read:

From: Maria@S.America.com

To: JB@U.Kingdom.com

Subject: Hasta La Vista.

Hi J.B.

How are you? ¿*Como Estas*? What a surprise! I am here in South America already and I hope you will be happy for me.

When the police took Sofia away I had to stay with her – she was so scared. But you were right, they did help us. They interrogated Sofia very well at the station and got back her *pasaporte*. Then they fixed a flight home for all the Earn As You Learn students also. I had to go back too – she was very preoccupated. It is so sad that we didn't have time to say goodbye properly.

The police told me that a newspaper man phoned them. That is why they were so quick and how they got R. English Jnr, too, and kept our families safe. Did you speak to the news man? If yes, it was the right thing to do. So, I must learn not to have a pig's head sometimes. (That is correct, non?)

I have told my family all about you. One day I hope you will come to visit me in my country. It is your destiny (or do I mean destination? I mix up). Until then please mail me.

Remember – words are our weapons.
Un beso
Maria X

I stare at the black-and-white screen. Stunned. If words are weapons then Maria's just cut me to pieces. She's gone. She's on the other side of the world. I can't believe it. I thought we were a crew.

I feel as empty as a rap without a rhyme. What about us? As in unfinished bizn-us? No word of a *lie*, I feel like I could *die*. (I must have something in my *eye*, 'cos rappers don't *cry*.)

Time out.

OK, now I don't just feel *sad*, I feel *mad*! Forget e-mailing her, she'll be hearing from my lawyers soon. Maria broke contract. I'll sue!

I press the DELETE button on the laptop and lay down on my bed. Time to rewrite the 'Revenge Rap' – it's gonna be remixed and re-released, the Full on, Xplicit version. Parents – you have been warned!

'J.B., are you in there?'

'Wh…what?'

I'm curled up on my bed, my mind as blank as the wall I've been staring at for the last hour.

Mum comes in, ignoring the sign on my door which clearly states:

Parental Advisory
- Keep outta my space
- Stay outta my face
- Know your place
- Don't...wear lace

She sits on my bed. 'Are you OK?'

'Yes.'

'Have you read Maria's e-mail?'

'Yes.'

'Are you going to answer it?'

'No.'

'Why not?'

'Nuthin' to say.'

She laughs. 'This from the boy who just won a rap contest and cut down two conmen with his sharp words!'

'Yeah well, that was different, I was part of a crew. Working with Maria made me think – I'm not a solo artist. So now she's left the country, I'm hanging up my mic.'

Mum sighs. 'Ah...I see. Well, at least Maria showed you there's life beyond Grimly – your school progress report says your Spanish has really improved.'

I should keep my mouth shut, I know, but there's still some of the old rapper spirit in me and the words are making a nasty taste in my mouth – I have to spit them out.

'She just...used me, Mum, to help Sofia. Then she...' *Wassup?* My voice is in fade-out mode and I've lost volume control, '...she dumped me and moved on...' I finish in a whisper.

Mum pats my arm and speaks gently. 'Don't be too hard on Maria, she didn't use you, Jamie. She really liked you, and you were there when she needed help. She was after the truth and together you found it, she won't forget that.'

I stop eyeballing the wall and turn round. Mum gives me one of her hard-act stares. 'Of course, you shouldn't have taken such a big risk,' she says, 'but that rap you did together was very special. Those words mattered. They made a difference.'

'*Hmmph*...' Mum's got this way of putting things, sometimes, so they stick in your mind. I wonder if she was a rapstar in her youth.

'Think about it,' she says and leaves, closing the door quietly after her.

I'm still confused... With Maria things came *clear*, I had a rap crew – and *career*. Now I've simply no *idea* (yo! It's hard to kick the rhyme habit).

I switch on the computer again and hesitate. Maria's mail is in the trash, but it hasn't been emptied yet.

Time for the final cut.

I press the bin icon and my finger hovers over the words EMPTY , then RESTORE .

It's a tough call. Shall I empty the trash and erase Maria from my memory for ever? I know she wants me to write but it's not like having her here with me. You can't kiss a computer screen. (OK, you can – but it can't kiss you back.)

Or shall I restore her e-mail and write back? Maria said, 'words are our weapons'. Mum said, 'words matter; they make a difference'. Ain't it da truth?

Hmm, maybe I *could* put some rhymes on-line and tap a keyboard-rap to Maria. It would be a big-time crime to waste my talent, after all! And if I learn Spanish, I could crack the Latin American rap market. Yo-le!

I press RESTORE.

Then REPLY – and start writing...

TURN THE PAGE TO READ
AN EXCITING EXTRACT FROM...

THE SECRET LIFE OF

JAMIE B

SUPERSPY

Ceri Worman

1 84362 389 7 £4.99

Oh yes, before I was J.B., the ravin'
Rapstar, I was Jamie B., International
Superspy, licensed to thrill. I was
working undercover at Albert's Autos.
OK, so a holiday job washing cars
wasn't exactly tracking subs in the
South Pacific, but there was definitely
something dodgy going on there...

CHAPTER 1

Shot by a Stun Gun

Hi – the name's B., Jamie B. International Secret Agent, licensed to thrill. If you want to know how to become a superspy then listen up! I'm going to tell you all about my new mission. There'll be action, danger, and love interest too... The question is, can you stand the pace?

A secret agent like me has only two basic states – asleep or alert. This morning I'm on *red* alert:

Jamie B. dives out of bed, checks his slippers for scorpions, then commando-rolls across the hall to avoid enemy sensors. In the bathroom, he whips back the shower curtain - FAST! but not fast enough. A robotic hit-man is already lunging towards him.

Metal Man's claws grab Jamie's throat in a grip of steel.

Is this the end for our hero?

With a supreme effort Jamie B. reaches across the sink for his supersonic soap bar and squeezes...

ZZZZaaPPP!

Burning acid bubbles explode over Metal Man. He staggers back clawing madly at his own throat.

Pop! Pop! Pop!

Each bursting bubble leaves a smoking hole of burning steel. Metal Man is dissolving faster than cyanide in champagne.

'I do hope you enjoyed your bubble bath,' says Jamie B.

Metal Man does not reply. He just disappears down the plughole in a slither of silvery slime.

Superspy B. sniffs at the soap bar. It's the first time he's tried this new gadget. Mmmmm! He'll be happy to report back to HQ that it's not only lethal, but lemony fresh too...

TO BE CONTINUED…

Orchard Red Apples

All books priced at £4.99

Orchard Red Apples are available from all good bookshops,
or can be ordered direct from the publisher:
Orchard Books, PO BOX 29, Douglas IM99 1BQ
Credit card orders please telephone 01624 836000 or fax 01624 837033
or visit our Internet site: www.wattspub.co.uk
or e-mail: bookshop@enterprise.net for details.

To order please quote title, author and ISBN
and your full name and address.
Cheques and postal orders should be made payable to 'Bookpost plc.'
Postage and packing is FREE within the UK
(overseas customers should add £1.00 per book).

Prices and availability are subject to change.